perfect
italian

Bath · New York · Singapore · Hong Kong · Cologne · Delhi · Melbourne

This is a Parragon Publishing book
First published in 2006

Parragon Publishing
Queen Street House
4 Queen Street
Bath BA1 1HE, UK

Copyright © Parragon Books Ltd 2006
Designed by Terry Jeavons & Company

ISBN 978-1-4075-1888-6

Printed in China

This book uses imperial, metric, and US cup measurements. Follow the same units of measurement throughout; do not mix imperial and metric. All spoon measurements are level, unless otherwise stated: teaspoons are assumed to be 5ml, and tablespoons are assumed to be 15ml. Unless otherwise stated, milk is assumed to be whole, eggs and individual fruits such as bananas are medium, and pepper is freshly ground black pepper.

Recipes using raw or very lightly cooked eggs should be avoided by infants, the elderly, pregnant women, convalescents, and anyone suffering from an illness. Pregnant and breast-feeding women are advised to avoid eating peanuts and peanut products.

Cover image: Italian Food Products © P. Hussenot/photocuisine/Corbis

perfect
italian

introduction

At the heart of Italian cuisine lies a very special ingredient – the legendary Italian love of good things, including good food. Learning the skills of cooking begins at an early age, as recipes and techniques are handed down the generations, and so too does an appreciation of well-prepared meals, whether a plate of *al dente* pasta topped with a simple sauce of freshly picked, sun-ripened tomatoes, a slow-cooked, aromatic beef stew, or a perfect seafood risotto.

It is often said that the essence of Italian cooking can be summed up in two words – seasonal and regional. Italians respect their ingredients and insist on the best quality, so they prefer to use

seasonal produce that, if possible, is locally grown. In provincial towns and villages, people shop daily for fresh produce in the markets and plan the day's menu around what looks, feels, and smells to be in peak condition.

This emphasis has had a lasting effect on the style of Italian cuisine, and simplicity is the key word. But simplicity means something different in each region of Italy. The reason for this is a mix of geographical and cultural diversity. The north of the country is cooler and wetter, while the south is hotter and drier, and the crops reflect this. In the north, dairy farming produces butter, cream, and cheese, which feature widely in the region's traditonal cooking, and both rice and maize are cultivated here, so risotto and polenta are staples. The south, on the other hand, is the home of pasta, olives and olive oil, tomatoes, eggplants, and citrus fruits.

The cultural differences arise from the fact that Italy has only

relatively recently become a unified "country," created from a number of independent states each with their own traditions, to which they adhere fiercely. This is perhaps part of the irresistible appeal of Italian cuisine – but whatever the reason, embrace it and enjoy it!

appetizers,
soups & salads

Soups are usually served as the first course of an Italian dinner, and they are so hearty and delicious that they also make excellent light lunch or supper dishes. Vegetables are the main ingredients of a good Italian soup, which sometimes has tiny soup pasta or rice added, occasionally a little meat, and frequently a selection of fish and seafood. The Italians are creative when it comes to adapting their soup recipes to include whatever vegetables are in season, and you can be, too.

If the soups are a visual feast, so too are the antipasti. They are a tasty, light, appetizing way to start a meal, consisting mainly of cured meats, vegetables, seafood, cheese, and salads. The ingredients are simple but the combinations effective – the three-color salad of fresh sliced tomatoes, buffalo mozzarella, and fragrant basil leaves is made in moments, and the superb Italian cured ham, prosciutto, is wonderful served with fresh fruit, such as melon or figs, or salad leaves such as arugula.

Olive oil makes a frequent appearance in the ingredients list for antipasto – save your best bottle of extra virgin olive oil for dressing salads or "drizzling" on hot dishes, as the excellent flavor will really enhance an authentic Italian dish. The slightly more acidic virgin olive oil can be used for cooking.

fresh tomato soup

ingredients

SERVES 4

1 tbsp. olive oil
1 lb 7 oz/650 g plum
    tomatoes
1 onion, cut into quarters
1 garlic clove, sliced thinly
1 celery stalk, chopped
    coarsely
18 fl oz/500 ml/generous
    2 cups chicken stock
2 oz/55 g dried anellini or
    other soup pasta
salt and pepper
fresh flat-leaf parsley,
    chopped, to garnish

method

Pour the olive oil into a large, heavy-bottom pan and add the tomatoes, onion, garlic, and celery. Cover and cook over low heat for 45 minutes, occasionally shaking the pan gently, until the mixture is pulpy.

Transfer the mixture to a food processor or blender and process to a smooth purée. Push the purée through a strainer into a clean pan.

Add the stock and bring to a boil. Add the pasta, bring back to a boil, and cook for 8–10 minutes, until the pasta is tender but still firm to the bite. Season to taste with salt and pepper. Ladle into warmed bowls, sprinkle with the parsley, and serve immediately.

minestrone

ingredients

SERVES 4

3 tbsp. olive oil

2 onions, chopped

1/2 small green or savoy
cabbage, thick stems
removed and leaves
shredded

2 zucchini, chopped

2 celery stalks, chopped

2 carrots, chopped

2 potatoes, chopped

4 large tomatoes, peeled
and chopped

4 oz/115 g dried Great
Northern beans, soaked
overnight in enough cold
water to cover

2 pints/1.2 litres/5 cups
chicken or
vegetable stock

4 oz/115 g dried soup pasta

salt and pepper

freshly shaved Parmesan
cheese, to garnish

4 tbsp. freshly grated
Parmesan cheese,
to serve

method

Heat the oil in a large heavy-bottomed pan. Add the
onions and cook over low heat, stirring occasionally,
for 5 minutes, or until softened.

Add the cabbage, zucchini, celery, carrots, potatoes, and
tomatoes to the pan, cover, and cook, stirring occasionally,
for 10 minutes.

Drain and rinse the beans, then add to the pan. Pour in the
stock, bring to a boil, cover, and simmer for 1–1^{1}/2 hours, or
until the beans are tender.

Add the soup pasta to the pan and cook, uncovered,
for 8–10 minutes, or until tender but still firm to the bite.
Season to taste with salt and pepper and ladle into
warmed bowls. Garnish with fresh Parmesan cheese
shavings and an extra sprinkling of pepper. Serve,
handing around the grated Parmesan cheese separately.

beef soup with eggs

ingredients

SERVES 4

for the consommé

1 lb 2 oz/500 g beef marrow
   bones, sawn into
   3-inch/7.5-cm pieces
12 oz/350 g stewing beef, in
   one piece
2½ pints/1.4 litres/6 cups
   water
4 cloves
2 onions, halved
2 celery stalks, chopped
   coarsely
8 peppercorns
1 bouquet garni

for the topping

2 oz/55 g unsalted butter
4 slices fresh white bread
4 oz/115 g/1 cup freshly
   grated Parmesan cheese
4 eggs
salt and pepper

method

First, make the consommé. Place the bones in a large, heavy-bottom pan with the stewing beef on top. Add the water and bring to a boil over low heat, skimming off all the scum that rises to the surface. Pierce a clove into each onion half and add to the pan with the celery, peppercorns, and bouquet garni. Partially cover and let simmer very gently for 3 hours. Remove the meat and let simmer for an additional hour.

Strain the consommé into a bowl and set aside to cool. When completely cool, let chill in the refrigerator for at least 6 hours, preferably overnight. Carefully remove and discard the layer of fat that has formed on the surface. Return the consommé to a clean pan and heat until almost boiling.

When you are ready to serve, melt the butter in a heavy-bottom skillet. Add the bread, 1 slice at a time if necessary, and cook over medium heat until crisp and golden on both sides. Remove from the skillet and place one each in the base of 4 warmed soup bowls.

Sprinkle half the Parmesan over the fried bread. Carefully break an egg over each slice of fried bread, keeping the yolks whole. Season to taste with salt and pepper and sprinkle with the remaining Parmesan. Carefully ladle the hot consommé into the soup bowls and serve immediately.

white bean soup

ingredients

SERVES 4

6 oz/175 g/1 cup dried
   cannellini beans, covered
   and soaked overnight in
   cold water
3 pints/1.7 litres/7 cups
   chicken or
   vegetable stock
4 oz/115 g dried corallini,
   conchigliette piccole,
   or other soup pasta
6 tbsp. olive oil
2 garlic cloves, chopped
   finely
4 tbsp. chopped fresh flat-leaf
   parsley
salt and pepper

method

Drain the soaked beans and place them in a large,
heavy-bottom pan. Add the stock and bring to a boil.
Partially cover the pan, reduce the heat, and let simmer
for 2 hours, until tender.

Transfer about half the beans and a little of the stock to
a food processor or blender and process to a smooth
purée. Return the purée to the pan and stir well to mix.
Bring the soup back to a boil.

Add the pasta to the soup, bring back to a boil and cook
for 10 minutes, until tender.

Meanwhile, heat 4 tablespoons of the olive oil in a small
pan. Add the garlic and cook over low heat, stirring
frequently, for 4–5 minutes, until golden. Stir the garlic
into the soup and add the parsley. Season to taste with
salt and pepper and ladle into warmed soup bowls. Drizzle
with the remaining olive oil and serve immediately.

genoese vegetable soup

ingredients

SERVES 8

2 onions, sliced

2 carrots, diced

2 celery stalks, sliced

2 potatoes, diced

4 oz/115 g green beans, cut
    into 1-inch/2.5-cm lengths

4 oz/115 g peas

7 oz/ 200 g fresh young
    spinach leaves, shredded

2 zucchini, diced

8 oz/225 g plum tomatoes,
    peeled, seeded, and diced

3 garlic cloves, sliced thinly

4 tbsp. extra-virgin olive oil

3^1/$_2$ pints/2 litres/8 cups
    vegetable stock

salt and pepper

5 oz/140 g dried soup pasta

freshly grated Parmesan
    cheese, to serve

for the pesto

4 tbsp. fresh basil leaves

1 tbsp. pine nuts

1 garlic clove

1 oz/25 g/^{1}/$_4$ cup freshly
    grated Parmesan cheese

3 tbsp. extra-virgin olive oil

method

Put the onions, carrots, celery, potatoes, beans, peas, spinach, zucchini, tomatoes, and garlic in a large, heavy-bottom pan, pour in the olive oil and stock, and bring to a boil over medium-low heat. Reduce the heat and let simmer gently for about 1^1/$_2$ hours.

Meanwhile, make the pesto. Put the basil, pine nuts, and garlic into a mortar and pound to a paste with a pestle. Transfer to a bowl and gradually work in the Parmesan with a wooden spoon, followed by the olive oil to make a thick, creamy sauce. Cover with plastic wrap and set aside in the refrigerator until required.

Season the soup to taste with salt and pepper and add the pasta. Cook for an additional 8–10 minutes, until the pasta is tender but still firm to the bite. The soup should be very thick. Stir in half the pesto, remove the pan from the heat and set aside to rest for 4 minutes. Taste and adjust the seasoning, adding more salt, pepper, and pesto if necessary. (Any leftover pesto may be stored in a screw-top jar in the refrigerator for up to 2 weeks.) Ladle into warmed bowls and serve immediately. Pass around the freshly grated Parmesan cheese separately.

mixed antipasto meat platter

ingredients

SERVES 4

1 cantaloupe

2 oz/55 g Italian salami, sliced
   thinly

8 slices prosciutto

8 slices bresaola

8 slices mortadella

4 plum tomatoes, sliced thinly

4 fresh figs, quartered

4 oz/115 g/2/3 cup black
   olives, pitted

2 tbsp. shredded fresh basil
   leaves

4 tbsp. extra-virgin olive oil,
   plus extra for serving

pepper

method

Cut the melon in half, scoop out and discard the seeds, then cut the flesh into 8 wedges. Arrange the wedges on one half of a large serving platter.

Arrange the salami, prosciutto, bresaola, and mortadella in loose folds on the other half of the platter. Arrange the tomato slices and fig quarters along the center of the platter.

Sprinkle the olives and shredded basil over the platter and drizzle with olive oil. Season to taste with pepper, then serve with extra olive oil.

marinated raw beef

ingredients

SERVES 4

7 oz/200 g fillet of beef, in
    one piece
2 tbsp. lemon juice
salt and pepper
4 tbsp. extra-virgin olive oil
2 oz/55g/1/2 cup Parmesan
    cheese, shaved thinly
4 tbsp. chopped fresh flat-leaf
    parsley
lemon slices, to garnish
ciabatta or focaccia, to serve

method

Using a very sharp knife, cut the beef fillet into wafer-thin slices and arrange on four individual serving plates.

Pour the lemon juice into a small bowl and season to taste with salt and pepper. Whisk in the olive oil, then pour the dressing over the meat. Cover the plates with plastic wrap and set aside for 10–15 minutes to marinate.

Remove and discard the plastic wrap. Arrange the Parmesan shavings in the center of each serving and sprinkle with parsley. Garnish with lemon slices and serve with fresh bread.

parma ham & figs

ingredients

SERVES 4

6 oz/175 g prosciutto,
   thinly sliced
pepper
4 fresh figs
1 lime
2 fresh basil sprigs

method

Using a sharp knife, trim the visible fat from the slices of prosciutto and discard. Arrange the prosciutto on 4 large serving plates, loosely folding it so that it falls into decorative shapes. Season to taste with pepper.

Using a sharp knife, cut each fig lengthwise into four wedges. Arrange a fig on each serving plate. Cut the lime into 6 wedges, place a wedge on each plate and reserve the others. Remove the leaves from the basil sprigs and divide between the plates. Cover with plastic wrap and let chill in the refrigerator until ready to serve.

Just before serving, remove the plates from the refrigerator and squeeze the juice from the remaining lime wedges over the ham.

prosciutto with arugula

ingredients

SERVES 4

4 oz/115 g arugula

1 tbsp. lemon juice

salt and pepper

3 tbsp. extra-virgin olive oil

8 oz/225 g prosciutto, sliced
   thinly

method

Separate the arugula leaves, wash in cold water, and pat dry on paper towels. Place the leaves in a bowl.

Pour the lemon juice into a small bowl and season to taste with salt and pepper. Whisk in the olive oil, then pour the dressing over the arugula leaves and toss lightly so they are evenly coated.

Carefully drape the prosciutto in folds on individual serving plates, then add the arugula. Serve at room temperature.

chicken crostini

ingredients

SERVES 4

12 slices French bread
  or rustic bread
4 tbsp. olive oil
2 garlic cloves, chopped
2 tbsp. finely chopped fresh
  oregano
salt and pepper
3¹/₂ oz/100 g cold roast
  chicken, cut into small,
  thin slices
4 tomatoes, sliced
12 thin slices of goat cheese
12 black olives, pitted and
  chopped
fresh red and green lettuce
  leaves, to serve

method

Preheat the oven to 350°F/180°C and the broiler to medium. Put the bread under the preheated broiler and lightly toast on both sides. Meanwhile, pour the olive oil into a bowl and add the garlic and oregano. Season with salt and pepper and mix well. Remove the toasted bread slices from the broiler and brush them on one side only with the oil mixture.

Place the bread slices, oiled sides up, on a cookie sheet. Put some sliced chicken on top of each one, followed by a slice of tomato. Divide the slices of goat cheese between them, then top with the chopped olives. Drizzle over the remaining oil mixture and transfer to the preheated oven. Bake for about 5 minutes, or until the cheese is golden and starting to melt. Remove from the oven and serve on a bed of fresh red and green lettuce leaves.

warm vegetable medley

ingredients

SERVES 4

4 tbsp. olive oil

2 celery stalks, sliced

2 red onions, sliced

450 g/1 lb eggplant, diced

1 garlic clove, chopped finely

5 plum tomatoes, chopped

3 tbsp. red wine vinegar

1 tbsp. sugar

3 tbsp. green olives, pitted

2 tbsp. capers

salt and pepper

4 tbsp. chopped fresh flat-leaf
    parsley

ciabatta or panini, to serve

method

Heat half the olive oil in a large, heavy-bottom pan. Add the celery and onions and cook over low heat, stirring occasionally, for 5 minutes, until softened but not colored. Add the remaining oil and the eggplant. Cook, stirring frequently, for about 5 minutes, until the eggplant starts to color.

Add the garlic, tomatoes, vinegar, and sugar, and mix well. Cover the mixture with a circle of waxed paper and let simmer gently for about 10 minutes.

Remove the waxed paper, stir in the olives and capers, and season to taste with salt and pepper. Pour the caponata into a serving dish and set aside to cool to room temperature. Sprinkle the parsley over the vegetables and serve with fresh bread or rolls.

sicilian stuffed tomatoes

ingredients

SERVES 4

8 large, ripe tomatoes

7 tbsp. extra-virgin olive oil

2 onions, finely chopped

2 garlic cloves, crushed

4 oz/115 g/2 cups fresh
   bread crumbs

8 anchovy fillets in oil,
   drained and chopped

3 tbsp. black olives, pitted
   and chopped

2 tbsp. chopped fresh flat-leaf
   parsley

1 tbsp. chopped fresh
   oregano

4 tbsp. freshly grated
   Parmesan cheese

method

Cut a thin slice off the tops of the tomatoes and discard. Scoop out the seeds with a teaspoon and discard, taking care not to pierce the shells. Turn the tomato shells upside down on paper towels to drain.

Heat 6 tablespoons of the olive oil in a skillet, add the onions and garlic, and cook over low heat, stirring occasionally, for 5 minutes, until softened. Remove the skillet from the heat and stir in the bread crumbs, anchovies, olives, and herbs.

Using a teaspoon, fill the tomato shells with the bread crumb mixture, then place in an ovenproof dish large enough to hold them in a single layer. Sprinkle the tops with grated Parmesan and drizzle with the remaining oil.

Bake in a preheated oven, 350°F/190°C, for 20–25 minutes, until the tomatoes are tender and the topping is golden brown.

Remove the dish from the oven and serve immediately, if serving hot, or let cool to room temperature.

roman artichokes

ingredients

SERVES 4

5 tbsp. lemon juice

4 globe artichokes

1 garlic clove

4 sprigs fresh flat-leaf parsley

2 sprigs fresh mint

1 lemon, quartered

4 tbsp. olive oil

salt and pepper

2 tbsp. dry, uncolored bread
   crumbs

2 garlic cloves, chopped finely

2 tbsp. fresh flat-leaf parsley,
   chopped coarsely

2 tbsp. fresh mint,
   chopped coarsely

1 tbsp. unsalted butter, diced

method

Fill a large bowl with cold water and 4 tablespoons of the lemon juice. Snap the stem off one artichoke, then peel away the tough outer leaves. Snip or break off the tough tops of the remaining leaves. Cut off the top $3/4$ inch/ 2 cm of the central cone with a sharp knife. Drop the artichoke into the bowl of water and prepare the others.

Wedge the artichokes firmly upright in a single layer in a heavy-bottom pan. Add the garlic clove, parsley sprigs, mint sprigs, lemon quarters, and olive oil, and season with salt and pepper. Pour in water to come two-thirds of the way up the sides. Bring to a boil over low heat, cover, and let simmer for 15 minutes, until nearly tender.

Combine the bread crumbs, chopped garlic, parsley, and mint in a bowl, and season with salt and pepper.

Remove the artichokes from the pan and set aside until cool enough to handle. Gently separate the leaves, then remove the central cones with a teaspoon and discard. Season the artichokes to taste with salt and pepper. Return them to the pan. Spoon the bread crumb mixture into the centers, cover tightly, and cook over low heat for 20–30 minutes, until tender. Remove with a slotted spoon and place on four individual plates.

Strain the cooking liquid into a clean pan and bring to a boil over high heat. Cook until the liquid is concentrated, then reduce the heat and stir in the remaining lemon juice. Add the butter, a piece at a time, swirling the sauce until the butter has melted. Do not let the sauce boil. Remove the pan from the heat. Serve the artichokes still warm and pass the sauce separately.

pasta salad with charbroiled bell peppers

ingredients

SERVES 4

1 red bell pepper

1 orange bell pepper

10 oz/280 g dried conchiglie

5 tbsp. extra-virgin olive oil

2 tbsp. lemon juice

2 tbsp. pesto (see page 16)

1 garlic clove

3 tbsp. shredded fresh basil
    leaves

salt and pepper

method

Put the whole bell peppers on a baking sheet and place under a preheated broiler, turning frequently, for 15 minutes, until charred all over. Remove with tongs and place in a bowl. Cover with crumpled paper towels and set aside.

Meanwhile, bring a large pan of lightly salted water to a boil. Add the pasta, bring back to a boil, and cook for 8–10 minutes, until tender but still firm to the bite.

Combine the olive oil, lemon juice, pesto, and garlic in a bowl, whisking well to mix. Drain the pasta, add it to the pesto mixture while still hot, and toss well. Set aside.

When the bell peppers are cool enough to handle, peel off the skins, then cut open and remove the seeds. Chop the flesh coarsely and add to the pasta with the basil. Season to taste with salt and pepper and toss well. Serve at room temperature.

warm pasta salad

ingredients

SERVES 4

8 oz/225 g dried farfalle or
   other pasta shapes
6 pieces of sun-dried tomato
   in oil, drained and chopped
4 scallions, chopped
2 oz/55 g arugula, shredded
1/2 cucumber, seeded and diced
2 tbsp. freshly grated
   Parmesan cheese
salt and pepper

dressing

4 tbsp. olive oil
1/2 tsp. superfine sugar
1 tbsp. white wine vinegar
1 tsp. Dijon mustard
4 fresh basil leaves,
   finely shredded
salt and pepper

method

To make the dressing, whisk the olive oil, sugar, vinegar, and mustard together in a bowl. Season to taste with salt and pepper. Stir in the basil.

Bring a large, heavy-bottom pan of lightly salted water to a boil. Add the pasta, return to a boil, and cook for 8–10 minutes, or until tender but still firm to the bite. Drain and transfer to a salad bowl. Add the dressing and toss well.

Add the chopped sun-dried tomatoes, scallions, arugula, and cucumber, season to taste with salt and pepper, and toss. Sprinkle with the Parmesan cheese and serve warm.

layered tomato salad

ingredients

SERVES 4

1 red onion, sliced thinly
   into rings
4 slices day-old bread
1 lb/450 g tomatoes, sliced
   thinly
4 oz/115 g mozzarella di
   bufala, sliced thinly
1 tbsp. shredded fresh basil
salt and pepper
4 fl oz/125 ml/$\frac{1}{2}$ cup extra-
   virgin olive oil
3 tbsp. balsamic vinegar
4 tbsp. lemon juice
4 oz/115 g/$\frac{2}{3}$ cup black
   olives, pitted and sliced
   thinly

method

Place the onion slices in a bowl and add cold water to cover. Set aside to soak for 10 minutes. Meanwhile, dip the slices of bread in a shallow dish of cold water, then squeeze out the excess. Place the bread in a serving dish.

Drain the onion slices and layer them on the bread with the tomatoes and mozzarella, sprinkling each layer with the basil and salt and pepper.

Pour over the olive oil, vinegar, and lemon juice, and sprinkle with the sliced olive. Cover and let chill for up to 8 hours before serving.

three-color salad

ingredients

SERVES 4

10 oz/280 g mozzarella di
    bufala, drained and
    sliced thinly
8 plum tomatoes, sliced
salt and pepper
20 fresh basil leaves
4 fl oz/125 ml/$^{1}/_{2}$ cup extra-
    virgin olive oil

method

Arrange the cheese and tomato slices on 4 individual serving plates and season to taste with salt. Set aside in a cool place for 30 minutes.

Sprinkle the basil leaves over the salad and drizzle with the olive oil. Season with pepper and serve immediately.

mozzarella salad with sun-dried tomatoes

ingredients

SERVES 4

5 oz/140 g sun-dried
tomatoes in olive oil
(drained weight),
reserving the oil from
the bottle

1 tbsp. fresh basil, shredded
coarsely

1 tbsp. fresh flat-leaf parsley,
chopped coarsely

1 tbsp. capers, rinsed

1 tbsp. balsamic vinegar

1 garlic clove, chopped
coarsely

extra olive oil, if necessary

pepper

3 1/2 oz/100 g mixed salad
greens, such as oak leaf
lettuce, baby spinach,
and arugula

1 lb 2 oz/500 g smoked
mozzarella, sliced

method

Put the sun-dried tomatoes, basil, parsley, capers, vinegar, and garlic in a food processor or blender. Measure the oil from the sun-dried tomatoes jar and add in enough oil to make 2/3 cup. Add it to the food processor or blender and process until smooth. Season to taste with pepper.

Divide the salad greens between 4 individual serving plates. Top with the slices of mozzarella and spoon the dressing over them. Serve immediately.

artichoke & rocket salad

ingredients

SERVES 4

8 baby globe artichokes

juice of 2 lemons

bunch of arugula

salt and pepper

4 fl oz/125 ml/1/2 cup extra-
   virgin olive oil

4 oz/115 g pecorino cheese

method

Break off the stems of the artichokes and cut off about 1 inch of the tops, depending on how young and small they are. Remove and discard any coarse outer leaves, leaving only the pale, tender inner leaves. Using a teaspoon, scoop out the chokes. Rub each artichoke with lemon juice as soon as it is prepared to prevent it from discoloring.

Thinly slice the artichokes and place in a salad bowl. Add the arugula, lemon juice, and olive oil, season to taste with salt and pepper, and toss well.

Using a swivel-blade vegetable peeler, thinly shave the pecorino over the salad, then serve immediately.

for meat lovers

Traditionally, wealthy Italians ate the best cuts of meat – often steak and veal – from animals raised on lush pastures, while their less well-off fellow countrymen tenderized the poorer cuts by long, slow cooking, resulting, as is so often the way, in some of the tastiest national dishes.

Veal is still very popular in Italy, and pork, lamb, beef, and poultry are also used in many different recipes. This chapter illustrates just a few of the ways in which meat can be used to bring a taste of Italy to your dining table – roasted, grilled, casseroled, pan-fried, combined with tomatoes and seasonings to make a thick, rich sauce for pasta dishes, or with the uniquely creamy-textured Italian rice to make risotto.

Many rural Italian families rear a pig each year for its meat, and any part that is not used for roasts, casseroles, stews, ham, and bacon is preserved as one of the many salamis, cured meats, and sausages for which Italy is famous. It is worth seeking out the appropriate type of Italian cured meat to use in a recipe – for example, pancetta, made from salted and spiced belly of pork, adds depth of flavor to spaghetti carbonara, a light pasta dish with a cream sauce, while luganega, a long, coiled pork sausage from northern Italy, works well with beans in a casserole.

spaghetti with meatballs

ingredients

SERVES 6

1 potato, diced
14 oz/400 g/1¾ cups
    ground steak
1 onion, finely chopped
1 egg
4 tbsp. chopped fresh flat-leaf
    parsley
all-purpose flour, for dusting
5 tbsp. virgin olive oil
14 fl oz/400 ml/1¾ cups
    strained tomatoes
2 tbsp. tomato paste
14 oz/400 g dried spaghetti
salt and pepper

for the garnish

6 fresh basil leaves, shredded
freshly grated Parmesan cheese

method

Place the potato in a small pan, add cold water to cover and a pinch of salt, and bring to a boil. Cook for 10–15 minutes, until tender, then drain. Either mash thoroughly with a potato masher or fork or pass through a potato ricer.

Combine the potato, steak, onion, egg, and parsley in a bowl and season to taste with salt and pepper. Spread out the flour on a plate. With dampened hands, shape the meat mixture into walnut-size balls and roll in the flour. Shake off any excess.

Heat the oil in a heavy-bottom skillet, add the meatballs, and cook over medium heat, stirring and turning frequently, for 8–10 minutes, until golden all over.

Add the strained tomatoes and tomato paste and cook for an additional 10 minutes, until the sauce is reduced and thickened.

Meanwhile, bring a large pan of lightly salted water to a boil. Add the pasta, bring back to a boil, and cook for 8–10 minutes, until tender but still firm to the bite.

Drain well and add to the meatball sauce, tossing well to coat. Transfer to a warmed serving dish, garnish with the basil leaves and Parmesan, and serve immediately.

spaghetti bolognese

ingredients

SERVES 4

2 tbsp. olive oil

1 tbsp. butter

1 small onion, finely chopped

1 carrot, finely chopped

1 celery stalk, finely chopped

1³/4 oz/50 g mushrooms, diced

8 oz/225 g ground beef

2³/4 oz/75 g unsmoked bacon
   or ham, diced

2 chicken livers, chopped

2 tbsp. tomato paste

14 fl oz/125 ml/¹/2 cup dry
   white wine

¹/2 tsp. freshly grated nutmeg

10 fl oz/300 ml/1¹/4 cups
   chicken stock

4 fl oz/125 ml/¹/2 cup heavy
   cream

1 lb/450 g dried spaghetti

salt and pepper

2 tbsp. chopped fresh
   flat-leaf parsley, to garnish

freshly grated Parmesan,
   to serve

method

Heat the olive oil and butter in a large pan over medium heat. Add the onion, carrot, celery, and mushrooms to the pan, then cook until soft. Add the beef and bacon and cook until the beef is evenly browned.

Stir in the chicken livers and tomato paste and cook for 2–3 minutes. Pour in the wine and season with salt, pepper, and the nutmeg. Add the stock. Bring to a boil, then cover and simmer gently over low heat for 1 hour. Stir in the cream and simmer, uncovered, until reduced.

Bring a large pan of lightly salted water to a boil. Add the pasta, return to a boil, and cook until tender but still firm to the bite. Drain and transfer to a warmed serving dish.

Spoon the meat sauce over the pasta, garnish with parsley, and serve with Parmesan cheese.

tagliatelle with a rich meat sauce

ingredients

SERVES 4

4 tbsp. olive oil, plus extra
   for serving
3 oz/85 g pancetta or rindless
   lean bacon, diced
1 onion, chopped
1 garlic clove, chopped finely
1 carrot, chopped
1 celery stalk, chopped
8 oz/225 g/1 cup ground
   steak
4 oz/225 g chicken livers,
   chopped
2 tbsp. strained tomatoes
4 fl oz/125 ml/1/2 cup dry
   white wine
8 fl oz/225 ml/1 cup beef
   stock or water
1 tbsp. chopped fresh
   oregano
1 bay leaf
salt and pepper
1 lb/450 g dried tagliatelle
freshly grated Parmesan
   cheese, to serve

method

Heat the olive oil in a large, heavy-bottom pan. Add the pancetta or bacon and cook over medium heat, stirring occasionally, for 3–5 minutes, until it is just turning brown. Add the onion, garlic, carrot, and celery and cook, stirring occasionally, for an additional 5 minutes.

Add the steak and cook over high heat, breaking up the meat with a wooden spoon, for 5 minutes, until browned. Stir in the chicken livers and cook, stirring occasionally, for an additional 2–3 minutes. Add the strained tomatoes, wine, stock, oregano, and bay leaf, and season to taste with salt and pepper. Bring to a boil, reduce the heat, cover, and simmer for 30–35 minutes.

When the sauce is almost cooked, bring a large pan of lightly salted water to a boil. Add the pasta, bring back to a boil, and cook for 8–10 minutes, until tender but still firm to the bite. Drain, transfer to a warmed serving dish, drizzle with a little olive oil, and toss well.

Remove and discard the bay leaf from the sauce, then pour it over the pasta, toss again, and serve immediately with grated Parmesan.

grilled steak with tomatoes & garlic

ingredients

SERVES 4

3 tbsp. olive oil, plus extra
     for brushing
1 lb 9 oz/700 g tomatoes,
     peeled and chopped
1 red bell pepper, seeded
     and chopped
1 onion, chopped
2 garlic cloves, chopped finely
1 tbsp. chopped fresh flat-leaf
     parsley
1 tsp. dried oregano
1 tsp. sugar
salt and pepper
4 6-oz/175-g entrecôte or
     rump steaks

method

Place the oil, tomatoes, red bell pepper, onion, garlic, parsley, oregano, and sugar in a heavy-bottom pan and season to taste with salt and pepper. Bring to a boil, reduce the heat, and let simmer for 15 minutes.

Meanwhile, trim any fat around the outsides of the steaks. Season each generously with pepper (but no salt) and brush with olive oil. Cook on a preheated grill pan according to taste: 2–3 minutes each side for rare; 3–4 minutes each side for medium 4–5 minutes on each side for well done.

Transfer the steaks to warmed individual plates and spoon the sauce over them. Serve immediately.

beef in red wine

ingredients

SERVES 4

2 lb 12 oz/1.25 kg topside
of beef

salt and pepper

3 tbsp. olive oil

1 red onion, chopped

1 garlic clove, chopped finely

2 carrots, sliced

2 celery stalks, sliced

1/2 fl oz/300 ml/1 1/4 cups
Chianti

7 oz/200 g canned
tomatoes, chopped

1 tbsp. chopped fresh oregano

1 tbsp. chopped fresh flat-leaf
parsley

1 bay leaf

method

Season the beef all over with salt and pepper. Heat the olive oil in a large, flameproof casserole. Add the beef and cook over medium heat, turning frequently, until browned on all sides. Use 2 large forks to remove the beef from the casserole.

Reduce the heat, add the onion, garlic, carrots, and celery, and cook, stirring occasionally, for 5 minutes, until softened. Pour in the wine and add the tomatoes, oregano, parsley, and bay leaf. Stir well to mix and bring to a boil.

Return the meat to the casserole and spoon the vegetable mixture over it. Cover and cook in a preheated oven, 350°F/180°C, spooning the vegetables over the meat occasionally, for 3–3 1/4 hours, until the beef is tender.

Transfer the beef to a carving board and cover with foil. Place the casserole on high heat and bring the juices to a boil. Continue to boil until reduced and thickened.

Carve the beef into slices and place on a warmed serving platter. Strain the thickened cooking juices over the beef and serve immediately.

baked lasagna

ingredients

SERVES 4

for the meat sauce

3 tbsp. olive oil

1 onion, chopped finely

1 celery stick, chopped finely

1 carrot, chopped finely

$3^1/2$ oz/100 g pancetta,
    chopped finely

6 oz/175 g/$^3/4$ cup
    ground beef

6 oz/175 g/$^3/4$ cup
    ground pork

$3^1/2$ fl oz/100 ml/scant
    $^1/2$ cup dry red wine

$^1/4$ pint/150 ml/$^2/3$ cup
    beef stock

1 tbsp. tomato paste

salt and pepper

1 clove

1 bay leaf

$^1/4$ pint/150 ml/$^2/3$ cup
    boiling milk

14 oz/400 g dried
    lasagna verdi

1 quantity béchamel sauce
    (see page 174)

5 oz/140 g mozzarella cheese

5 oz/140 g freshly grated
    Parmesan cheese

2 oz/55 g unsalted butter,
    diced

method

First, make the meat sauce. Heat the olive oil in a large, heavy-bottom pan. Add the onion, celery, carrot, pancetta, beef, and pork, and cook over medium heat, stirring frequently and breaking up the meat with a wooden spoon, for 10 minutes, until lightly browned.

Add the wine, bring to a boil, and cook until reduced. Add about two-thirds of the stock, bring to a boil, and cook until reduced. Combine the remaining stock and tomato paste and add to the pan. Season to taste, add the clove, the bay leaf, and pour in the milk. Cover and let simmer over low heat for $1^1/2$ hours.

Unless you are using lasagna that needs no precooking, bring a large pan of lightly salted water to a boil. Add the lasagna sheets, in batches, bring back to a boil, and cook for about 10 minutes, until tender but still firm to the bite. Remove with tongs and spread out on a clean dish towel.

Remove the meat sauce from the heat and discard the clove and bay leaf. Lightly grease a large, oven-proof dish with butter. Place a layer of the pasta in the base and cover it with a layer of meat sauce. Spoon a layer of béchamel sauce on top and sprinkle with one-third of the mozzarella and Parmesan cheeses. Continue making layers until all the ingredients are used, ending with a topping of béchamel sauce and sprinkled cheese.

Dot the top of the lasagna with the diced butter and bake in a preheated oven, 400°F/200°C, for 30 minutes, until golden and bubbling.

meatball surprise

ingredients

SERVES 8

1 lb 2 oz/500 g ground steak

1 lb 2 oz/500 g ground pork

2 garlic cloves, chopped
   finely

2 oz/55 g/1 cup fresh bread
   crumbs

1³/₄ oz/50 g/scant ¹/₂ cup
   freshly grated Parmesan
   cheese

1 tsp. dried oregano

¹/₂ tsp. ground cinnamon

grated rind and juice of
   1 lemon

2 eggs, beaten lightly

5¹/₂ oz/150 g fontina cheese

6 tbsp. virgin olive oil

5 oz/140 g/1¹/₄ cups dried,
   uncolored bread crumbs

salt and pepper

fresh flat-leaf parsley sprigs,
   to garnish

tomato sauce (see page 80),
   to serve

method

Combine the steak, pork, garlic, fresh bread crumbs, Parmesan, oregano, cinnamon, and lemon rind in a bowl. Stir in the lemon juice and beaten eggs, season with salt and pepper, and mix well.

Knead the mixture with dampened hands, then shape small quantities into 16 balls.

Cut the fontina into 16 cubes and press 1 cube into each meatball, then reshape them to enclose the cheese completely.

Heat the olive oil in a large, heavy-bottom skillet. Meanwhile, spread out the dried bread crumbs on a shallow plate and roll the meatballs in them to coat.

Add the meatballs, in batches, to the skillet and cook until golden brown all over. Transfer to an ovenproof dish using a slotted spoon and bake in a preheated oven, 350°F/180°C, for 15–20 minutes, until cooked through. Serve immediately, garnished with parsley sprigs and accompanied with tomato sauce.

pan-fried pork with mozzarella

ingredients

SERVES 4

1 lb/450 g loin of pork

2–3 garlic cloves, chopped
   finely

6 oz/175 g mozzarella di
   bufala, drained

salt and pepper

12 slices prosciutto

12 fresh sage leaves

2 oz/55 g unsalted butter

mostarda di Verona, to serve
   (optional)

flat-leaf parsley sprigs

lemon slices, to garnish

method

Trim any excess fat from the meat, then slice it crosswise into 12 pieces, each about 1 inch thick. Stand each piece on end and beat with the flat end of a meat mallet or the side of a rolling pin until thoroughly flattened. Rub each piece all over with garlic, transfer to a plate, and cover with plastic wrap. Set aside in a cool place for 30 minutes to 1 hour.

Cut the mozzarella into 12 slices. Season the pork to taste with salt and pepper, then place a slice of cheese on top of each slice of meat. Top with a slice of prosciutto, letting it fall in folds. Place a sage leaf on each portion and secure with a toothpick.

Melt the butter in a large, heavy-bottom skillet. Add the pork, in batches if necessary, and cook for 2–3 minutes on each side, until the meat is tender and the cheese has melted. Remove with a slotted spoon and keep warm while you cook the remaining batch.

Remove and discard the toothpicks. Transfer the pork to 4 warmed individual plates, garnish with parsley and lemon slices, and serve immediately with mostarda di Verona.

pork fillets with fennel

ingredients

SERVES 4

1 lb/450 g pork fillet

2–3 tbsp. virgin olive oil

2 tbsp. sambuca

1 large fennel bulb, sliced, fronds reserved

3 oz/85 g Gorgonzola cheese, crumbled

2 tbsp. light cream

1 tbsp. chopped fresh sage

1 tbsp. chopped fresh thyme

salt and pepper

method

Trim any fat from the pork and cut into ¼-inch-thick slices. Place the slices between 2 sheets of plastic wrap and beat with the flat end of a meat mallet or with a rolling pin to flatten slightly.

Heat 2 tablespoons of the oil in a heavy-bottom skillet and add the pork, in batches. Cook over medium heat for 2–3 minutes on each side, until tender. Remove from the skillet and keep warm. Cook the remaining batches, adding more oil if necessary.

Stir the sambuca into the skillet, increase the heat, and cook, stirring constantly and scraping up the glazed bits from the bottom. Add the fennel and cook, stirring and turning frequently, for 3 minutes. Remove from the skillet and keep warm.

Reduce the heat, add the Gorgonzola and cream, and cook, stirring constantly, until smooth. Remove the skillet from the heat, stir in the sage and thyme, and season to taste with salt and pepper.

Divide the pork and fennel between 4 warmed individual serving plates and pour over the sauce. Garnish with the reserved fennel fronds and serve immediately.

pork and pasta bake

ingredients

SERVES 4

2 tbsp. olive oil

1 onion, chopped

1 garlic clove, finely chopped

2 carrots, diced

2 oz/55 g pancetta, chopped

4 oz/115 g mushrooms,
   chopped

1 lb/450 g ground pork

4 fl oz/125 ml/1/2 cup dry
   white wine

4 tbsp. strained canned
   tomatoes

7 oz/200 g canned chopped
   tomatoes

2 tsp. chopped fresh sage

8 oz/225 g dried elicoidali

5 oz/140 g mozzarella
   cheese, diced

4 tbsp. freshly grated
   parmesan cheese

10 fl oz/300 ml/1 1/4 cups
   hot béchamel sauce
   (see page 174)

salt and pepper

method

Preheat the oven to 400°F/200°C. Heat the olive oil in a large, heavy-bottom skillet. Add the onion, garlic, and carrots and cook over low heat, stirring occasionally, for 5 minutes, or until the onion has softened. Add the pancetta and cook for 5 minutes. Add the chopped mushrooms and cook, stirring occasionally, for an additional 2 minutes. Add the pork and cook, breaking it up with a wooden spoon, until the meat is browned all over. Stir in the wine, strained tomatoes, chopped tomatoes and their can juices, and sage. Season to taste with salt and pepper and bring to a boil, then cover and simmer over low heat for 25–30 minutes.

Meanwhile, bring a large, heavy-bottom pan of lightly salted water to a boil. Add the pasta, return to a boil, and cook for 8–10 minutes, or until tender but still firm to the bite.

Spoon the pork mixture into a large ovenproof dish. Stir the mozzarella and half the Parmesan cheese into the béchamel sauce. Drain the pasta and stir the sauce into it, then spoon it over the pork mixture. Sprinkle with the remaining Parmesan cheese and bake in the oven for 25–30 minutes, or until golden brown.
Serve immediately.

spicy pork risotto

ingredients

SERVES 4

1³/₄ pints/1 litre/4 cups
    simmering beef stock
    (see page 76)

1 thick slice white bread,
    crust removed and
    discarded

water or milk, for soaking

1 lb/450 g fresh ground pork

2 garlic cloves, minced

1 tbsp. finely chopped onion

1 tsp. black peppercorns,
    lightly crushed

pinch of salt

1 egg

corn oil, for pan-frying

14 oz/400 g canned chopped
    tomatoes

1 tbsp. tomato paste

1 tsp. dried oregano

1 tsp. fennel seeds

pinch of sugar

3 tbsp butter

1 tbsp. olive oil

1 small onion, finely chopped

10 oz/280 f/generous 1³/₈
    cups risotto rice

5 fl oz/150 ml/²/₃ cup
    red wine

salt and pepperfresh basil
    leaves, to garnish

method

Soak the bread in the water or milk for 5 minutes to soften. Drain and squeeze well to remove all the liquid. Mix the bread, pork, garlic, onion, crushed peppercorns, and salt together in a bowl. Add the egg and mix well.

Heat the corn oil in a skillet over medium heat. Form the meat mixture into balls and cook a few at a time until browned. Remove each batch from the skillet and drain.

Combine the tomatoes, tomato paste, oregano, fennel seeds, and sugar in a heavy-bottom pan. Add the meatballs. Bring the sauce to a boil over medium heat, then reduce the heat and let simmer for 30 minutes, or until the meat is thoroughly cooked.

Meanwhile, melt 2 tablespoons of the butter with the olive oil n a deep pan over medium heat. Stir in the onion and cook, stirring occasionally, for 5 minutes, or until soft and starting to turn golden. Do not brown.

Reduce the heat, add the rice, and mix to coat in oil and butter. Cook, stirring constantly, for 2–3 minutes, or until the grains are translucent.

Add the wine and cook, stirring constantly, for 1 minute until reduced. Gradually add the hot stock, a ladleful at a time. Stir constantly and add more liquid as the rice absorbs each addition. Increase the heat to medium so that the liquid bubbles. Cook for 20 minutes, or until all the liquid is absorbed. Season to taste.

Lift out the cooked meatballs and add to the risotto. Remove from the heat and add the remaining butter. Mix well. Arrange the risotto and meatballs on plates. Drizzle with tomato sauce, garnish with basil, and serve.

cannelloni with spinach & ricotta

ingredients

SERVES 4

12 dried cannelloni tubes,
   3-in long
butter, for greasing

for the filling

5 oz/140 g lean ham,
   chopped
5 oz/140 g/3/4 cup frozen
   spinach, thawed and
   drained
4 oz/115 g/scant 1/2 cup
   ricotta cheese
1 egg
3 tbsp. freshly grated pecorino
   cheese
pinch of freshly grated nutmeg
salt and pepper

for the cheese sauce

1 pint/600 ml/21/2 cups milk
1 oz/25 g unsalted butter
2 tbsp. all-purpose flour
3 oz/85 g/3/4 cup freshly
   grated Gruyère cheese
salt and pepper

method

Bring a large pan of lightly salted water to a boil. Add the cannelloni tubes, bring back to a boil, and cook for 6–7 minutes, until nearly tender. Drain and rinse under cold water. Spread out the tubes on a clean dish towel.

Put the ham, spinach, and ricotta into a food processor and process for a few seconds until combined. Add the egg and pecorino and process again to a smooth paste. Scrape the filling into a bowl and season to taste with nutmeg, salt, and pepper.

Grease an ovenproof dish with butter. Spoon the filling into a pastry bag fitted with a 1/2-inch nozzle. Carefully open one cannelloni tube, stand it upright, and pipe in the filling. Place the filled tube in the dish and continue to fill the remaining cannelloni.

To make the cheese sauce, heat the milk to just below boiling point. Meanwhile, melt the butter in another pan. Add the flour to the butter and cook over low heat, stirring constantly, for 1 minute. Remove the pan from the heat and gradually stir in the hot milk. Return the pan to the heat and bring to a boil, stirring constantly. Let simmer over the lowest possible heat, stirring frequently, for 10 minutes, until thickened and smooth. Remove the pan from the heat, stir in the Gruyère, and season to taste with salt and pepper.

Spoon the cheese sauce over the filled cannelloni. Cover the dish with foil and bake in a preheated oven, 350°F/180°C, for 20–25 minutes. Serve immediately.

spaghetti alla carbonara

ingredients

SERVES 4

1 lb/450 g dried spaghetti

1 tbsp. olive oil

8 oz/225 g rindless pancetta
   or lean bacon, chopped

4 eggs

5 tbsp. light cream

4 tbsp. freshly grated
   Parmesan cheese

salt and pepper

method

Bring a large, heavy-bottom pan of lightly salted water to a boil. Add the pasta, return to a boil, and cook for 8–10 minutes, or until tender but still firm to the bite.

Meanwhile, heat the olive oil in a heavy-bottom skillet. Add the chopped pancetta and cook over medium heat, stirring frequently, for 8–10 minutes.

Beat the eggs with the cream in a small bowl and season to taste with salt and pepper. Drain the pasta and return it to the pan. Tip in the contents of the skillet, then add the egg mixture and half the Parmesan cheese. Stir well, then transfer to a warmed serving dish. Serve immediately, sprinkled with the remaining Parmesan cheese.

sausages with cranberry beans

ingredients

SERVES 4

2 tbsp. virgin olive oil

1 lb 2 oz/500 g luganega or other Italian sausage

5 oz/140 g smoked pancetta or lean bacon, diced

2 red onions, chopped

2 garlic cloves, chopped finely

8 oz/225 g/1⅓ cups dried cranberry beans, covered and soaked overnight in cold water

2 tsp. finely chopped fresh rosemary

2 tsp. chopped fresh sage

10 fl oz/300 ml/1¼ cups dry white wine

salt and pepper

fresh rosemary sprigs, to garnish

crusty bread, to serve

method

Heat the oil in a flameproof casserole. Add the sausages and cook over low heat, turning frequently, for about 10 minutes, until browned all over. Remove from the casserole and set aside.

Add the pancetta to the casserole, increase the heat to medium and cook, stirring frequently, for 5 minutes, or until golden brown. Remove with a slotted spoon and set aside.

Add the onions to the casserole and cook over low heat, stirring occasionally, for 5 minutes, until softened. Add the garlic and cook for an additional 2 minutes.

Drain the beans and set aside the soaking liquid. Add the beans to the casserole, then return the sausages and pancetta. Gently stir in the herbs and pour in the wine. Measure the reserved soaking liquid and add 1¼ cups to the casserole. Season to taste with salt and pepper. Bring to a boil over low heat and boil for 15 minutes, then transfer to a preheated oven, 275°F/140°C, and cook for 2¾ hours.

Remove the casserole from the oven and ladle the sausages and beans onto 4 warmed serving plates. Garnish with the rosemary sprigs and serve immediately with crusty bread.

sausage & rosemary risotto

ingredients

SERVES 4–6

2¼ pints/1.3 litres/generous
    5½ cups simmering
    chicken stock (*see
    method)
2 long fresh rosemary sprigs,
    plus extra to garnish
2 tbsp. olive oil
2 oz/55 g butter
1 large onion, finely chopped
1 celery stalk, finely chopped
2 garlic cloves, finely chopped
½ tsp dried thyme leaves
1 lb/450 g pork sausage,
    such as luganega or
    cumberland, cut into
    ½-inch/1-cm pieces
12 oz/350 g/generous 1⅝
    cups risotto rice
4 fl oz/125 ml/½ cup fruity
    red wine
3 oz/85 g/¾ cup freshly
    grated Parmesan cheese
salt and pepper

method

*Bring the stock to a boil in a pan, then reduce the heat and keep simmering gently over low heat while you are cooking the risotto.

Strip the long thin leaves from the rosemary sprigs and chop finely, then set aside.

Heat the oil and half the butter in a deep pan over medium heat. Add the onion and celery and cook, stirring occasionally, for 2 minutes. Stir in the garlic, thyme, sausage, and rosemary. Cook, stirring frequently, for 5 minutes, or until the sausage starts to brown. Transfer the sausage to a plate.

Reduce the heat, add the rice, and mix to coat in oil and butter. Cook, stirring constantly, for 2–3 minutes, or until the grains are translucent.

Add the wine and cook, stirring constantly, for 1 minute until reduced. Gradually add the hot stock, a ladleful at a time. Stir constantly and add more liquid as the rice absorbs each addition. Increase the heat to medium so that the liquid bubbles. Cook for 20 minutes, or until all the liquid is absorbed and the rice is creamy.

Toward the end of cooking, return the sausage pieces to the risotto and heat through. Season to taste with salt and pepper.

Remove from the heat and add the remaining butter. Mix well, then stir in the Parmesan until it melts. Spoon the risotto onto warmed plates, garnish with rosemary sprigs, and serve.

pepperoni pasta

ingredients

SERVES 4

3 tbsp. olive oil

1 onion, chopped

1 red bell pepper, seeded and
    diced

1 orange bell pepper, seeded
    and diced

1 lb 12 oz/800 g canned
    chopped tomatoes

1 tbsp. sun-dried tomato paste

1 tsp. paprika

8 oz/225 g pepperoni, sliced

2 tbsp. chopped fresh
    flat-leaf parsley, plus extra
    to garnish

1 lb/450 g dried garganelli

salt and pepper

mixed salad greens,
    to serve

method

Heat 2 tablespoons of the olive oil in a large, heavy-bottom
skillet. Add the onion and cook over low heat, stirring
occasionally, for 5 minutes, or until softened. Add the red
and orange bell peppers, tomatoes and their can juices,
sun-dried tomato paste, and paprika to the pan and bring
to a boil.

Add the pepperoni and parsley and season to taste with
salt and pepper. Stir well and bring to a boil, then reduce
the heat and simmer for 10–15 minutes.

Meanwhile, bring a large, heavy-bottom pan of lightly
salted water to a boil. Add the pasta, return to a boil,
and cook for 8–10 minutes, or until tender but still firm
to the bite. Drain well and transfer to a warmed serving
dish. Add the remaining olive oil and toss. Add the sauce
and toss again. Sprinkle with parsley and serve immediately
with mixed salad greens.

four seasons pizza

ingredients

SERVES 2

pizza dough (see page 200)

plain flour, for dusting

for the tomato sauce

2 tbsp. olive oil

1 small onion, chopped finely

1 garlic clove, chopped finely

1 red bell pepper, seeded and chopped

8 oz/225 g plum tomatoes, peeled and chopped

1 tbsp. tomato paste

1 tsp. soft brown sugar

1 tbsp. shredded fresh basil

1 bay leaf

salt and pepper

for the topping

2¹/₂ oz cooked shrimp

2 oz bottled artichoke hearts, sliced thinly

1 oz mozzarella cheese, drained and sliced thinly

1 tomato, sliced thinly

3¹/₂ oz/100 g mushrooms or pepperoni, sliced thinly

2 tsp. capers, rinsed

2 tsp. pitted, sliced black olives

2 tbsp. olive oil

salt and pepper

method

To make the tomato sauce, heat the olive oil in a heavy-bottom pan. Add the onion, garlic, and bell pepper, and cook over low heat, stirring occasionally, for 5 minutes, until softened. Add the tomatoes, tomato paste, sugar, basil, and bay leaf, and season to taste with salt and pepper. Cover and let simmer, stirring occasionally, for 30 minutes, until thickened. Remove the pan from the heat and let the sauce cool completely.

Turn out the prepared pizza dough onto a lightly floured counter and knock down. Knead briefly, then cut it in half and roll out each piece into a circle about ¹/₄ inch/0.75 cm thick. Transfer to a lightly oiled baking sheet and push up the edges with your fingers to form a small rim.

Spread the tomato sauce over the pizza bases, almost to the edge. Cover one-quarter with shrimp. Cover a second quarter with sliced artichoke hearts. Cover the third quarter with alternate slices of mozzarella and tomato. Cover the final quarter with sliced mushrooms or pepperoni. Sprinkle the surface with capers and olives, season to taste with salt and pepper, and drizzle with the olive oil.

Bake in a preheated oven, 425°F/220°C, for 20–25 minutes, until the crust is crisp and the cheese has melted.

Serve immediately.

roast lamb with rosemary & marsala

ingredients

SERVES 6

4 lb/1.8 kg leg of lamb
2 garlic cloves, sliced thinly
2 tbsp. rosemary leaves
8 tbsp. olive oil
salt and pepper
2 lb/900 g potatoes, cut into
    1-inch/2.5-cm cubes
6 fresh sage leaves, chopped
1/4 pint/150 ml/2/3 cup
    Marsala

method

Use a small, sharp knife to make incisions all over the lamb, opening them out slightly to make little pockets. Insert the garlic slices and about half the rosemary leaves in the pockets.

Place the lamb in a roasting pan and spoon half the olive oil over it. Roast in a preheated oven, 425°F/220°C, for 15 minutes. Reduce the oven temperature to 350°F/180°C. Remove the lamb from the oven and season to taste with salt and pepper. Turn the lamb over, return to the oven, and roast for an additional hour.

Meanwhile, spread out the cubed potatoes in a second roasting pan, pour the remaining olive oil over them, and toss to coat. Sprinkle with the remaining rosemary and the sage. Place the potatoes in the oven with the lamb and roast for 40 minutes.

Remove the lamb from the oven, turn it over, and pour over the Marsala. Return it to the oven with the potatoes and cook for an additional 15 minutes.

Transfer the lamb to a carving board and cover with foil. Place the roasting pan over high heat and bring the juices to a boil. Continue to boil until thickened and syrupy. Strain into a warmed gravy boat or pitcher. Carve the lamb into slices and serve with the potatoes and sauce.

lamb shanks with roasted onions

ingredients

SERVES 4

4 12-oz/350 g lamb shanks

6 garlic cloves

2 tbsp. virgin olive oil

1 tbsp. very finely chopped
  fresh rosemary

salt and pepper

4 red onions

12 oz/350 g carrots, cut into
  thin sticks

4 tbsp. water

method

Trim off any excess fat from the lamb. Using a small, sharp knife, make 6 incisions in each shank. Cut the garlic cloves lengthwise into 4 slices. Insert 6 garlic slices in the incisions in each lamb shank.

Place the lamb in a single layer in a roasting pan, drizzle with the olive oil, sprinkle with the rosemary, and season with pepper. Roast in a preheated oven, 350°F/180°C, for 45 minutes.

Wrap each onion in a square of foil. Remove the lamb shanks from the oven and season with salt. Return the pan to the oven and place the onions on the shelf next to it. Roast for an additional 1 hour, or until the lamb is tender.

Meanwhile, bring a large pan of water to a boil. Add the carrot sticks and blanch for 1 minute. Drain and refresh under cold water.

Remove the roasting pan from the oven when the lamb is meltingly tender and transfer it to a warmed serving dish. Skim off any fat from the roasting pan and place it over medium heat. Add the carrots and cook for 2 minutes, then add the water, bring to a boil, and let simmer, stirring constantly and scraping up the glazed bits from the bottom of the roasting pan.

Transfer the carrots and sauce to the serving dish. Remove the onions from the oven and unwrap. Cut off and discard about 1/2 inch/1.25 cm of the tops and add the onions to the dish. Serve immediately.

spicy lamb with black olives

ingredients

SERVES 6

6 tbsp. olive oil

1 onion, chopped

2 garlic cloves, chopped finely

2 lb 12 oz/1.25 kg boneless
   leg of lamb, cut into
   1-inch/2.5-cm cubes

2 dried whole peperoncini or
   other red chilies

6 fl oz/175 ml/3/4 cup dry
   white wine

6 oz/175 g/1 cup black olives,
   pitted

2 tbsp. chopped fresh flat-leaf
   parsley, plus extra to garnish

salt

method

Heat the olive oil in a large, flameproof casserole. Add the onion and garlic and cook over low heat, stirring occasionally, for 5 minutes, until softened.

Add the cubed lamb and cook, stirring frequently, for 5 minutes, until browned all over. Crumble in the chilies, pour in the wine, and cook for an additional 5 minutes. Stir in the olives and parsley and season to taste with salt.

Transfer the casserole to a preheated oven, 350°F/180°C, and cook for 1 1/2 hours, until the lamb is tender. Garnish with extra parsley and serve immediately.

hot pepper lamb in red wine risotto

ingredients

SERVES 4

4 fl oz/125 ml/5 cups
  simmering chicken stock
  (see page 76)

4 tbsp. all-purpose flour,
  seasoned with salt
  and pepper

8 pieces neck of lamb

4 tbsp. olive oil

1 green bell pepper, seeded
  and thinly sliced

1–2 fresh green chilies,
  seeded and thinly sliced

1 small onion, thinly sliced

1 small onion, finely chopped

2 garlic cloves, thinly sliced

2 tbsp. torn fresh basil

4 fl oz/125 ml/1/2 cup
  red wine

4 tbsp. red wine vinegar

8 cherry tomatoes

4 fl oz/125 ml/1/2 cup water

3 tbsp. butter

10 oz/280 g/generous 13/8
  cups risotto rice

3 oz/85 g/3/4 cup freshly
  grated Parmesan cheese

salt and pepper

method

Spread the flour on a plate. Coat the lamb in the flour, shaking off any excess. Heat 3 tablespoons of the oil in a large casserole over high heat. Add the lamb and cook until browned. Remove from the casserole and set aside.

Lightly brown the bell pepper, chilies, sliced onion, garlic, and basil in the casserole. Add the wine and vinegar, bring to a boil, and cook over high heat for 3–4 minutes until the liquid is reduced to 2 tablespoons.

Add the tomatoes and the water, stir, and bring to a boil. Return the meat, cover, and reduce the heat to low. Cook for 30 minutes, or until the meat is tender.

Meanwhile, melt 2 tablespoons of the butter with the remaining oil in a deep pan over medium heat. Add the chopped onion and cook, stirring occasionally, for 5 minutes, or until soft and starting to turn golden. Do not brown. Reduce the heat, add the rice, and mix to coat in oil and butter. Cook, stirring constantly, for 2–3 minutes, or until the grains are translucent.

Gradually add the hot stock, a ladleful at a time. Stir constantly and add more liquid as the rice absorbs each addition. Increase the heat to medium so that the liquid bubbles. Cook for 20 minutes, or until all the liquid is absorbed and the rice is creamy. Season to taste.

Remove the risotto from the heat and add the remaining butter. Mix well, then stir in the Parmesan until it melts. Arrange a scoop of risotto on each plate and sprinkle with peppers and tomatoes. Top with the lamb and serve.

veal with prosciutto & sage

ingredients

SERVES 4

4 veal scallops

2 tbsp. lemon juice

salt and pepper

1 tbsp. chopped fresh
   sage leaves

4 slices prosciutto

2 oz/55 g unsalted butter

3 tbsp. dry white wine

method

Place the veal scallops between 2 sheets of plastic wrap and pound with the flat end of a meat mallet or the side of a rolling pin until very thin. Transfer to a plate and sprinkle with the lemon juice. Set aside for 30 minutes, spooning the juice over them occasionally.

Pat the scallops dry with paper towels, season with salt and pepper, and rub with half the sage. Place a slice of prosciutto on each scallop and secure with a toothpick.

Melt the butter in a large, heavy-bottom skillet. Add the remaining sage and cook over low heat, stirring constantly, for 1 minute. Add the scallops and cook for 3–4 minutes on each side, until golden brown. Pour in the wine and cook for an additional 2 minutes.

Transfer the scallops to a warmed serving dish and pour the pan juices over them. Remove and discard the toothpicks and serve immediately.

milanese veal

ingredients

SERVES 4

1 tbsp. virgin olive oil

4 tbsp. butter

2 onions, chopped

1 leek, chopped

3 tbsp. all-purpose flour

salt and pepper

4 thick slices of veal shin
(osso bucco)

1/2 pint/300 ml/11/4 cups
white wine

1/2 pint/300 ml/11/4 cups veal
or chicken stock

for the gremolata

2 tbsp. chopped fresh parsley

1 garlic clove, chopped finely

grated rind of 1 lemon

method

Heat the oil and butter in a large, heavy-bottom skillet. Add the onions and leek and cook over low heat, stirring occasionally, for 5 minutes, until softened.

Spread out the flour on a plate and season with salt and pepper. Toss the pieces of veal in the flour to coat, shaking off any excess. Add the veal to the skillet, increase the heat to high, and cook until browned on both sides.

Gradually stir in the wine and stock and bring just to a boil, stirring constantly. Reduce the heat, cover, and let simmer for 11/4 hours, or until the veal is very tender.

Meanwhile, make the gremolata by mixing the parsley, garlic, and lemon rind in a small bowl.

Transfer the veal to a warmed serving dish with a slotted spoon. Bring the sauce to a boil and cook, stirring occasionally, until thickened and reduced. Pour the sauce over the veal, sprinkle with the gremolata, and serve immediately.

tuscan chicken

ingredients

SERVES 4

2 tbsp. all-purpose flour

salt and pepper

4 skinned chicken quarters or portions

3 tbsp. olive oil

1 red onion, chopped

2 garlic cloves, chopped finely

1 red bell pepper, seeded and chopped

pinch of saffron threads

1/4 pint/150 ml/2/3 cup chicken stock or a mixture of chicken stock and dry white wine

14 oz/400 g canned tomatoes, chopped

4 sun-dried tomatoes in oil, drained and chopped

8 oz/225 g portobello mushrooms, sliced

4 oz/115 g/2/3 cup black olives, pitted

4 tbsp. lemon juice

fresh basil leaves, to garnish

method

Place the flour on a shallow plate and season with salt and pepper. Coat the chicken in the seasoned flour, shaking off any excess. Heat the olive oil in a large, flameproof casserole. Add the chicken and cook over medium heat, turning frequently, for 5–7 minutes, until golden brown. Remove from the casserole and set aside.

Add the onion, garlic, and red bell pepper to the casserole, reduce the heat and cook, stirring occasionally, for 5 minutes, until softened. Meanwhile, stir the saffron into the stock.

Stir the tomatoes with the juice from the can, the sun-dried tomatoes, mushrooms, and olives into the casserole and cook, stirring occasionally, for 3 minutes. Pour in the stock and saffron mixture and the lemon juice. Bring to a boil, then return the chicken to the casserole.

Cover and cook in a preheated oven, 350°F/180°C, for 1 hour, until the chicken is tender. Garnish with the basil leaves and serve immediately.

pappardelle with chicken & porcini

ingredients

SERVES 4

1½ oz/40 g dried porcini
mushrooms

6 fl oz/170 ml/¾ cup hot
water

1 lb 12 oz/800 g canned
chopped tomatoes

1 fresh red chili, seeded and
finely chopped

3 tbsp. olive oil

12 oz/350 g skinless, boneless
chicken, cut into thin strips

2 garlic cloves,
finely chopped

12 oz/350 g dried
pappardelle

salt and pepper

2 tbsp. chopped fresh
flat-leaf parsley, to garnish

method

Place the porcini in a small bowl, add the hot water, and let soak for 30 minutes. Meanwhile, place the tomatoes and their can juices in a heavy-bottom pan and break them up with a wooden spoon, then stir in the chili. Bring to a boil, then reduce the heat and simmer, stirring occasionally, for 30 minutes, or until reduced.

Remove the mushrooms from their soaking liquid with a slotted spoon, reserving the liquid. Strain the liquid through a coffee filter paper or cheesecloth-lined strainer into the tomatoes and simmer for an additional 15 minutes. Meanwhile, heat 2 tablespoons of the olive oil in a heavy-bottom skillet. Add the chicken and cook, stirring frequently, until golden brown all over and tender. Stir in the mushrooms and garlic and cook for an additional 5 minutes.

While the chicken is cooking, bring a large, heavy-bottom pan of lightly salted water to a boil. Add the pasta, return to a boil, and cook for 8–10 minutes, or until tender but still firm to the bite. Drain well, then transfer to a warmed serving dish. Drizzle the pasta with the remaining olive oil and toss lightly. Stir the chicken mixture into the tomato sauce, season to taste with salt and pepper, and spoon onto the pasta. Toss lightly, sprinkle with parsley, and serve immediately.

creamy chicken ravioli

ingredients

SERVES 4

4 oz/115 g cooked skinless,
   boneless chicken breast,
   coarsely chopped

2 oz/55 g cooked spinach

2 oz/55 g prosciutto, coarsely
   chopped

1 shallot, coarsely chopped

6 tbsp. freshly grated romano
   cheese

pinch of freshly grated nutmeg

2 eggs, lightly beaten

1 quantity basic pasta dough
   (see page 164, omitting
   spinach from the recipe)

all-purpose flour, for dusting

10 fl oz/300 ml/1¼ cups
   heavy cream or panna
   da cucina

2 garlic cloves, finely chopped

4 oz/115 g cremini mushrooms,
   thinly sliced

2 tbsp. shredded fresh basil

salt and pepper

fresh basil sprigs, to garnish

method

Place the chicken, spinach, prosciutto, and shallot in a food processor and process until chopped and blended. Transfer to a bowl, stir in 2 tablespoons of the romano cheese, the nutmeg, and half the egg. Season to taste with salt and pepper.

Halve the pasta dough. Wrap one piece in plastic wrap and thinly roll out the other on a lightly floured counter. Cover with a dish towel and roll out the second piece of dough. Place small mounds of the filling in rows 1½ inches/4 cm apart on one sheet of dough and brush the spaces in between with beaten egg. Lift the second piece of dough to fit on top. Press down firmly between the mounds of filling, pushing out any air. Cut into squares and place on a floured dish towel. Let the ravioli rest for 1 hour.

Bring a large pan of lightly salted water to a boil. Add the ravioli, in batches, return to a boil, and cook for 5 minutes. Remove with a slotted spoon and drain on paper towels, then transfer to a warmed dish.

Meanwhile, to make the sauce, pour the cream into a skillet, add the garlic, and bring to a boil. Simmer for 1 minute, then add the mushrooms and 2 tablespoons of the remaining cheese. Season to taste and simmer for 3 minutes. Stir in the basil, then pour the sauce over the ravioli. Sprinkle with the remaining cheese, garnish with basil sprigs, and serve.

chicken tortellini

ingredients

SERVES 4

4 oz/115 g boned chicken
    breast, skinned
2 oz/55 g prosciutto
$1^1/_2$ oz/40 g cooked spinach,
    well drained
1 tbsp. finely chopped onion
2 tbsp. freshly grated
    Parmesan cheese
pinch of ground allspice
1 egg, beaten
1 lb/450 g basic pasta dough
    (see page 164, omitting
    spinach from the recipe)
salt and pepper
2 tbsp. chopped fresh
    parsley, to garnish

sauce

10 fl oz/300 ml/$1^1/_4$ cups
    light cream
2 garlic cloves, crushed
4 oz/115 g white mushrooms,
    thinly sliced
4 tbsp. freshly grated
    Parmesan cheese

method

Bring a pan of salted water to a boil. Add the chicken and poach for about 10 minutes. Let cool slightly, then place in a food processor with the prosciutto, spinach, and onion and process until finely chopped. Stir in the Parmesan cheese, allspice, and egg and season with salt and pepper to taste.

Thinly roll out the pasta dough and cut into $1^1/_2$–2-inch/ 4–5-cm circles.

Place $^1/_2$ teaspoon of the chicken and ham filling in the center of each circle. Fold the pieces in half and press the edges to seal, then wrap each piece round your index finger, cross over the ends, and curl the rest of the dough backward to make a navel shape. Re-roll the trimmings and repeat until all of the dough is used up.

Bring a pan of salted water to a boil. Add the tortellini, in batches, return to a boil and cook for 5 minutes. Drain the tortellini well and transfer to a serving dish.

To make the sauce, bring the cream and garlic to a boil in a small pan, then simmer for 3 minutes. Add the mushrooms and half of the cheese, season to taste with salt and pepper, and simmer for 2–3 minutes. Pour the sauce over the tortellini. Sprinkle over the remaining Parmesan cheese, garnish with the parsley, and serve.

chicken, mushroom & cashew risotto

ingredients

SERVES 4

2¼ pints/1.3 litre//generous
    5½ cups simmering
    chicken stock (see
    page 76)
2 oz/55 g butter
1 onion, chopped
9 oz/250 g skinless, boneless
    chicken breasts, diced
12 oz/350 g/generous
    1⅝ cups risotto rice
1 tsp ground turmeric
5 fl oz/150 ml/⅔ cup
    white wine
2¾ oz/75 g cremini
    mushrooms, sliced
1¾ oz/50 g/scant ⅓ cup
    cashews, halved
salt and pepper

to garnish

wild arugula
fresh Parmesan
    cheese shavings
fresh basil leaves

method

Melt the butter in a large pan over medium heat. Add the onion and cook, stirring occasionally, for 5 minutes, or until softened. Add the chicken and cook, stirring frequently, for an additional 5 minutes.

Reduce the heat, add the rice, and mix to coat in butter. Cook, stirring constantly, for 2–3 minutes, or until the grains are translucent.

Stir in the turmeric, then add the wine. Cook, stirring constantly, for 1 minute until reduced.

Gradually add the hot stock, a ladleful at a time. Stir constantly and add more liquid as the rice absorbs each addition. Increase the heat to medium so that the liquid bubbles. Cook for 20 minutes, or until all the liquid is absorbed and the rice is creamy.

About 3 minutes before the end of the cooking time, stir in the mushrooms and cashews. Season to taste.

Arrange the arugula leaves on 4 individual serving plates. Remove the risotto from the heat and spoon it over the arugula. Sprinkle over the Parmesan shavings and basil leaves and serve.

risotto with char-grilled chicken breast

ingredients

SERVES 4

1³/4 pints/1 litre/4 cups
   simmering chicken stock
   (see page 76)
4 boneless chicken breasts,
   about 4 oz/115 g each,
   seasoned with salt and
   pepper
grated rind and juice of
   1 lemon
5 tbsp. olive oil
1 garlic clove, crushed
8 fresh thyme sprigs,
   finely chopped
3 tbsp. butter
1 small onion, finely chopped
10 oz/280 g/generous
   1³/8 cups risotto rice
5 fl oz/150 ml/²/3 cup dry
   white wine
3 oz/85 g/³/4 cup freshly
   grated parmesan or Grana
   padano cheese
salt and pepper

to garnish

lemon wedges
fresh thyme sprigs

method

Place the chicken in a shallow, nonmetallic dish. Combine the lemon rind and juice, 4 tablespoons of the olive oil, the garlic, and thyme in a bowl and rub into the chicken. Cover with plastic wrap and let marinate in the refrigerator for 4–6 hours. Return the chicken to room temperature.

Preheat a grill pan over high heat. Add the chicken, skin-side down, and cook for 10 minutes, or until the skin is crisp and starting to brown. Turn over and brown the underside. Reduce the heat and cook for an additional 10–15 minutes, or until the juices run clear. Let rest on a carving board for 5 minutes, then cut into thick slices.

Meanwhile, heat 2 tablespoons of the butter with the remaining oil in a deep pan over medium heat. Add the onion and cook, stirring occasionally, for 5 minutes, or until soft and starting to turn golden. Reduce the heat, add the rice, and mix to coat in oil and butter. Cook, stirring, for 2–3 minutes, or until the grains are translucent. Add the wine and cook, stirring, for 1 minute until reduced.

Gradually add the hot stock, a ladleful at a time. Stir constantly and add more liquid as the rice absorbs each addition. Increase the heat to medium so that the liquid bubbles. Cook for 20 minutes, or until all the liquid is absorbed and the rice is creamy. Season to taste.

Remove the risotto from the heat and add the remaining butter. Mix well, then stir in the Parmesan until it melts. Put a scoop of risotto on each plate, add the chicken slices, garnish with lemon and thyme and serve at once.

for seafood fans

Almost surrounded by sea, and with its many lakes and rivers, it is not surprising that Italy has a tradition of cooking and eating fine fish. Generations of Italian cooks have perfected the art of preparing and cooking fish and seafood in recipes that bring out their flavor and texture to perfection.

Unfortunately, what was once an inexpensive or even free source of food is rapidly becoming a luxury item because marine pollution and over-enthusiastic fishing have resulted in stocks being depleted. However, there are still some species of saltwater fish that are not found elsewhere and are often only available in preserved form. Anchovies, for example, are rarely seen fresh outside the Mediterranean, but the canned or salted versions (rinsed well before use) are useful for adding a distinctive flavor to pasta sauces, pizzas, and salads. Tuna is another Mediterranean favorite, a large, oily fish that is fabulous cut into fresh steaks, and a very versatile store-cupboard item canned in oil or brine.

Other Italian favorites include swordfish, red mullet, sea bream, sea bass, sardines, and shellfish, as well as freshwater fish such as trout. If you are a seafood fan, try cooking your own favorite in the Italian style – delicious and nutritious.

red mullet with capers and olives

ingredients

SERVES 4

1 lb 9 oz/700 g red snapper
  fillets (about 12)

3 tbsp. chopped fresh marjoram
  or flat-leaf parsley

thinly peeled rind of 1 orange,
  cut into thin strips

8 oz/225 g mixed salad
  greens, torn into pieces

6 fl oz/175 ml/3/4 cup extra-
  virgin olive oil

1 tbsp. balsamic vinegar

1 tbsp. white wine vinegar

1 tsp. Dijon mustard

salt and pepper

3 tbsp. virgin olive oil

1 fennel bulb, cut into thin
  sticks

for the sauce

1 tbsp. butter

11/2 oz/40 g/1/4 cup black
  olives, pitted and
  sliced thinly

1 tbsp. capers, rinsed

method

Place the fish fillets on a large plate, sprinkle with the marjoram, and season with salt and pepper. Set aside.

Blanch the orange rind in a small pan of boiling water for 2 minutes, drain, refresh under cold water, and drain well again.

Place the mixed salad greens in a large bowl. Whisk together the extra-virgin olive oil, balsamic vinegar, wine vinegar, and mustard in a small bowl and season to taste with salt and pepper. Alternatively, shake all the dressing ingredients in a screw-top jar. Pour the dressing over the salad greens and toss well. Arrange the salad leaves on a large serving platter to make a bed.

Heat the virgin olive oil in a large, heavy-bottom skillet. Add the fennel and cook, stirring constantly, for 1 minute. Remove the fennel with a slotted spoon, set aside, and keep warm. Add the fish fillets, skin-side down, and cook for 2 minutes. Carefully turn them over and cook for an additional 1–2 minutes. Remove from the skillet and drain on paper towels. Keep warm.

To make the sauce, melt the butter in a small pan, add the olives and capers, and cook, stirring constantly, for 1 minute.

Place the fish fillets on the bed of salad greens, top with the orange rind and fennel, and pour over the sauce or pass it around separately in a warmed pitcher. Serve immediately.

roast sea bream with fennel

ingredients

SERVES 4

9 oz/250 g/2¼ cups dried, uncolored bread crumbs

2 tbsp. milk

1 fennel bulb, sliced thinly, fronds reserved for garnish

1 tbsp. lemon juice

2 tbsp. sambuca

1 tbsp. chopped fresh thyme

1 bay leaf, crumbled

3 lb 5 oz/1.5 kg whole sea bream, cleaned, scaled, and boned

salt and pepper

3 tbsp. olive oil, plus extra for brushing

1 red onion, chopped

½ pint/300 ml/1¼ cups dry white wine

method

Place the bread crumbs in a bowl, add the milk, and set aside for 5 minutes to soak. Place the fennel in another bowl and add the lemon juice, sambuca, thyme, and bay leaf. Squeeze the bread crumbs and add them to the mixture, stirring well.

Rinse the fish inside and out under cold running water and pat dry with paper towels. Season with salt and pepper. Spoon the fennel mixture into the cavity, then bind the fish with trussing thread or kitchen string.

Brush a large ovenproof dish with olive oil and sprinkle the onion over the bottom. Lay the fish on top and pour in the wine—it should reach about one-third of the way up the fish. Drizzle the sea bream with the olive oil and cook in preheated oven, 475°F/240°C, for 25–30 minutes. Baste the fish occasionally with the cooking juices and if it starts to brown, cover with a piece of foil to protect it.

Carefully lift out the fish, remove the string, and place on a warmed serving platter. Garnish with the reserved fennel fronds and serve immediately.

swordfish with olives & capers

ingredients

SERVES 4

2 tbsp. all-purpose flour

salt and pepper

4 8-oz/225 g swordfish steaks

3 1/2 fl oz/100 ml/generous
   1/3 cup olive oil

2 garlic cloves, halved

1 onion, chopped

4 anchovy fillets, drained and
   chopped

4 tomatoes, peeled, seeded,
   and chopped

12 green olives, pitted and
   sliced

1 tbsp. capers, rinsed

fresh rosemary leaves,
   to garnish

method

Spread out the flour on a plate and season with salt and pepper. Coat the fish in the seasoned flour, shaking off any excess.

Gently heat the olive oil in a large, heavy-bottom skillet. Add the garlic and cook over low heat for 2–3 minutes, until just golden. Do not let it turn brown or burn. Remove the garlic and discard.

Add the fish to the skillet and cook over medium heat for about 4 minutes on each side, until cooked through and golden brown. Remove the steaks from the skillet and set aside.

Add the onion and anchovies to the skillet and cook, mashing the anchovies with a wooden spoon until they have turned to a purée and the onion is golden. Add the tomatoes and cook over low heat, stirring occasionally, for about 20 minutes, until the mixture has thickened.

Stir in the olives and capers and taste and adjust the seasoning. Return the steaks to the skillet and heat through gently. Serve garnished with rosemary.

trout in lemon & red wine sauce

ingredients

SERVES 4

4 trout, cleaned, heads
    removed
8 fl oz/225 ml/1 cup
    red wine vinegar
1/2 pint//300 ml/11/4 cups
    red wine
1/4 pint//150 ml/2/3 cup water
2 bay leaves
4 sprigs fresh thyme
4 sprigs fresh flat-leaf parsley,
    plus extra to garnish
thinly pared rind of 1 lemon
3 shallots, sliced thinly
1 carrot, sliced thinly
12 black peppercorns
8 cloves
salt
3 oz/85 g unsalted butter,
    diced
1 tbsp. chopped fresh flat-leaf
    parsley
1 tbsp. snipped fresh dill
salt and pepper

method

Rinse the fish inside and out under cold running water and pat dry on paper towels. Place them in a single layer in a nonmetallic dish. Pour the vinegar into a small pan and bring to a boil, then pour it over the fish. Set aside to marinate for 30 minutes.

Pour the wine and water into a pan, add the bay leaves, thyme sprigs, parsley sprigs, lemon rind, shallots, carrots, peppercorns, and cloves, and season with salt. Bring to a boil over low heat.

Meanwhile, drain the trout and discard the vinegar. Place the fish in a single layer in a large skillet and strain the wine mixture over them. Cover and let simmer over low heat for 15 minutes, until cooked through and tender. There is no need to turn them.

Using a spatula, transfer the trout to individual serving plates and keep warm. Bring the cooking liquid back to a boil and cook until reduced by about three-quarters. Gradually beat in the butter, a little at a time, until fully incorporated. Stir in the chopped parsley and dill and taste adjust the seasoning if necessary. Pour the sauce over the fish, garnish with parsley sprigs, and serve immediately.

grilled sardines with lemon sauce

ingredients

SERVES 4

1 large lemon

3 oz/85 g unsalted butter

salt and pepper

20 fresh sardines, cleaned
and heads removed

1 tbsp. chopped fresh fennel
leaves

method

Peel the lemon. Remove all the bitter pith and discard. Using a small, serrated knife, cut between the membranes and ease out the flesh segments, discarding any seeds. Chop finely and set aside.

Melt 1 oz/28 g of the butter in a small pan and season with salt and pepper. Brush the sardines all over with the melted butter and cook under a preheated broiler or on a barbecue, turning once, for 5–6 minutes, until cooked through.

Meanwhile, melt the remaining butter, then remove the pan from the heat. Stir in the chopped lemon and fennel.

Transfer the sardines to a warmed platter, pour the sauce over them, and serve immediately.

linguine with anchovies, olives & capers

ingredients

SERVES 4

for the sauce

3 tbsp. olive oil

2 garlic cloves, chopped finely

10 anchovy fillets, drained
    and chopped

5 oz/140 g/scant 1 cup black
    olives, pitted and chopped

1 tbsp. capers, rinsed

1 lb/450 g plum tomatoes,
    peeled, seeded, and
    chopped

pinch of cayenne pepper

salt

14 oz/400 g dried linguine

2 tbsp. chopped fresh flat-leaf
    parsley, to garnish

method

Heat the olive oil in a heavy-bottom pan. Add the garlic and cook over low heat, stirring frequently, for 2 minutes. Add the anchovies and mash them to a pulp with a fork. Add the olives, capers, and tomatoes and season to taste with cayenne pepper. Cover and let simmer for 25 minutes.

Meanwhile, bring a pan of lightly salted water to a boil. Add the pasta, bring back to a boil, and cook for 8–10 minutes, until tender but still firm to the bite. Drain and transfer to a warmed serving dish.

Spoon the anchovy sauce into the dish and toss the pasta, using 2 large forks. Garnish with the parsley and serve immediately.

fillets of sole in tomato & olive sauce

ingredients

SERVES 4

4 tbsp. olive oil

2 lb/900 g plum tomatoes, peeled, seeded, and chopped

2 tbsp. sun-dried tomato paste

3 garlic cloves, chopped finely

1 tbsp. chopped fresh oregano

salt and pepper

3 oz/85 g/generous 1/2 cup all-purpose flour

4 sole, filleted

3 oz/85 g unsalted butter

4 oz/115 g/2/3 cup black olives, pitted

method

Heat the olive oil in a large, heavy-bottom pan. Add the tomatoes, tomato paste, garlic, and oregano, and season with salt and pepper. Stir well, then cover and let simmer, stirring occasionally, for 30 minutes, until the mixture is thickened and pulpy.

Meanwhile, spread out the flour on a plate and season with salt and pepper. Coat the fish fillets in the seasoned flour, shaking off any excess.

Melt half the butter in a heavy-bottom skillet. Add as many fillets as the skillet will hold in a single layer and cook over medium heat for 2 minutes on each side. Using a spatula, transfer the fillets to an ovenproof dish and keep warm. Cook the remaining fillets, adding the remaining butter as required.

Stir the olives into the tomato sauce, then pour it over the fish. Bake in a preheated oven, 350°F/180°C, for 20 minutes. Serve immediately, straight from the dish.

risotto with sole & tomatoes

ingredients

SERVES 4

2 pints/1.2 litres/5 cups
   simmering fish or chicken
   stock (see page 76)
3 tbsp. butter
3 tbsp. olive oil
1 small onion, finely chopped
10 oz/280 g/generous
   1³/₈ cups risotto rice
1 lb/450 g tomatoes, peeled,
   seeded, and cut into strips
6 sun-dried tomatoes
   in olive oil, drained and
   thinly sliced
3 tbsp. tomato paste
2 fl oz/50 ml/¹/₄ cup red wine
1 lb/450 g sole or flounder
   fillets, skinned
4 oz/115 g/1 cup freshly
   grated Parmesan or Grana
   Padano cheese
salt and pepper
2 tbsp. finely chopped fresh
   cilantro, to garnish

method

Melt 2 tablespoons of the butter with 1 tablespoon of the oil in a deep pan over medium heat. Stir in the onion and cook, stirring occasionally, for 5 minutes, or until soft and starting to turn golden. Reduce the heat, add the rice, and mix to coat in butter and oil. Cook, stirring constantly, for 2–3 minutes, or until the grains are translucent.

Gradually add the hot stock, a ladleful at a time. Stir constantly and add more liquid as the rice absorbs each addition. Increase the heat to medium so that the liquid bubbles. Cook for 20 minutes, or until all the liquid is absorbed and the rice is creamy. Season to taste.

Meanwhile, heat the remaining oil in a large, heavy-bottom skillet. Add the fresh and dried tomatoes. Stir well and cook over medium heat for 10–15 minutes, or until soft and slushy. Stir in the tomato paste and wine. Bring the sauce to a boil, then reduce the heat until it is just simmering.

Cut the fish into strips and add to the sauce. Stir gently. Cook for 5 minutes, or until the fish flakes when checked with a fork. Most of the liquid should be absorbed, but if it isn't, remove the fish and then increase the heat to reduce the sauce.

Remove the risotto from the heat when all the liquid has been absorbed and add the remaining butter. Mix well, then stir in the Parmesan until it melts.

Place the risotto on serving plates and arrange the fish and sauce on top. Garnish with fresh cilantro and serve.

sicilian tuna

ingredients

SERVES 4

4 5-oz/140 g tuna steaks
2 fennel bulbs, sliced thickly
    lengthwise
2 red onions, sliced
2 tbsp. virgin olive oil
crusty rolls, to serve

for the marinade

4 fl oz/125 ml/$^1/_2$ cup
    extra-virgin olive oil
4 garlic cloves, chopped finely
4 fresh red chilies, seeded
    and chopped finely
juice and finely grated rind of
    2 lemons
4 tbsp. finely chopped fresh
    flat-leaf parsley
salt and pepper

method

First, make the marinade by whisking all the ingredients together in a bowl. Place the tuna steaks in a large shallow dish and spoon over 4 tablespoons of the marinade, turning to coat. Cover and set aside for 30 minutes. Set aside the remaining marinade.

Heat a ridged grill pan. Put the fennel and onions in a bowl, add the oil, and toss well to coat. Add to the grill pan and cook for 5 minutes on each side, until just starting to color. Transfer to 4 warmed serving plates, drizzle with the reserved marinade, and keep warm.

Add the tuna steaks to the grill pan and cook, turning once, for 4–5 minutes, until firm to the touch but still moist inside. Transfer the tuna to the plates and serve immediately with crusty bread.

beans with tuna

ingredients

SERVES 4

1 lb 12 oz/800 g Great
    Northern beans, covered
    and soaked overnight in
    cold water
6 tbsp. extra-virgin olive oil
2 7-oz/200-g tuna steaks
2 garlic cloves, crushed lightly
sprig fresh sage
2 tbsp. water
salt and pepper
4 chopped fresh sage leaves,
    to garnish

method

Drain the soaked beans and place them in a pan. Add enough water to cover and bring to a boil. Reduce the heat and let simmer for 1–1$\frac{1}{2}$ hours, until tender. Drain the beans thoroughly.

Heat 1 tablespoon of the olive oil in a heavy-bottom skillet. Add the tuna steaks and cook over medium heat for 3–4 minutes on each side, until tender. Remove from the skillet and set aside to cool.

Heat 3 tablespoons of the remaining olive oil in a heavy-bottom skillet. Add the garlic and sage sprig and cook briefly over low heat until the sage starts to sizzle. Remove the garlic and discard.

Add the beans and cook for 1 minute, then add the measured water and season to taste with salt and pepper. Cook until the water has been absorbed. Remove and discard the sage sprig, transfer the beans to a bowl, and set aside to cool.

Meanwhile, flake the tuna, removing any bones. When the beans are lukewarm or at room temperature, according to taste, gently stir in the tuna. Drizzle with the remaining olive oil, sprinkle with the chopped sage, and serve.

seafood omelet

ingredients

SERVES 3

2 tbsp. unsalted butter

1 tbsp. olive oil

1 onion, chopped very finely

6 oz/175 g zucchini, halved
lengthwise and sliced

1 celery stalk, chopped
very finely

3 oz/85 g white mushrooms,
sliced

2 oz/55 g green beans, cut
into 2-in lengths

4 eggs

3 oz/85 g/3/8 cup
mascarpone cheese

1 tbsp. chopped fresh thyme

1 tbsp. shredded fresh basil

salt and pepper

7 oz/200 g canned tuna,
drained and flaked

4 oz/115 g shelled cooked
shrimp

method

Melt the butter with the olive oil in a heavy-bottom skillet with a flameproof handle. If the skillet has a wooden handle, protect it with foil because it needs to go under the broiler. Add the onion and cook over low heat, stirring occasionally, for 5 minutes, until softened.

Add the zucchini, celery, mushrooms, and beans and cook, stirring occasionally, for an additional 8–10 minutes, until starting to brown.

Beat the eggs with the mascarpone, thyme, basil, and salt and pepper to taste.

Add the tuna to the skillet and stir it into the mixture with a wooden spoon. Add the shrimp last.

Pour the egg mixture into the skillet and cook for 5 minutes, until it is just starting to set. Draw the egg from the sides of the skillet toward the center to let the uncooked egg run underneath.

Put the skillet under a preheated broiler and cook until the egg is just set and the surface is starting to brown. Cut the omelet into wedges and serve.

tuna with garlic, lemon, capers & olives

ingredients

SERVES 4

12 oz/350 g/3 cups dried
    conchiglie or gnocchi

4 tbsp. olive oil

4 tbsp. butter

3 large garlic cloves, sliced
    thinly

7 oz/200 g canned tuna, drained
    and broken into chunks

2 tbsp. lemon juice

1 tbsp capers, drained

10–12 black olives, pitted
    and sliced

2 tbsp. chopped fresh
    flat-leaf parsley, to serve

method

Cook the pasta in plenty of boiling salted water until al dente. Drain and return to the pan.

Heat the olive oil and half the butter in a skillet over a medium–low heat. Add the garlic and cook for a few seconds, or until just beginning to color. Reduce the heat to low. Add the tuna, lemon juice, capers, and olives. Stir gently until all the ingredients are heated through.

Transfer the pasta to a warm serving dish. Pour the tuna mixture over the pasta. Add the parsley and remaining butter. Toss well to mix. Serve immediately.

risotto with tuna & pine nuts

ingredients

SERVES 4

2 pints/1.2 litres/5 cups
   simmering fish or chicken
   stock (see page 76)
3 tbsp. butter
4 tbsp. olive oil
1 small onion, finely chopped
10 oz/280 g/generous 1³/₈
   cups risotto rice
8 oz/225 g tuna, canned
   and drained, or broiled
   fresh steaks
8–10 black olives, pitted and
   sliced
1 small pimiento, thinly sliced
1 tsp. finely chopped
   fresh parsley
1 tsp. finely chopped
   fresh marjoram
2 tbsp. white wine vinegar
2 oz/55 g/³/₈ cup pine nuts
1 garlic clove, chopped
8 oz/225 g fresh tomatoes,
   peeled, seeded, and diced
3 oz/85 g/³/₄ cup Parmesan
   or Grana Padano cheese
salt and pepper

method

Melt 2 tablespoons of the butter with 1 tablespoon of the oil in a deep pan over medium heat. Add the onion and cook, stirring, for 5 minutes, or until soft and starting to turn golden. Reduce the heat, add the rice, and mix to coat in butter and oil. Cook, stirring constantly, for 2–3 minutes, or until the grains are translucent.

Gradually add the stock, a ladleful at a time. Stir constantly and add more liquid as the rice absorbs each addition. Increase the heat to medium so that the liquid bubbles. Cook for 20 minutes until all the liquid is absorbed and the rice is creamy. Season to taste.

While the risotto is cooking, flake the tuna into a bowl and mix in the olives, pimiento, parsley, marjoram, and vinegar. Season to taste.

Heat the remaining oil in a small skillet over high heat. Add the pine nuts and garlic. Cook, stirring constantly, for 2 minutes, or until they just start to brown.

Add the tomatoes to the skillet and mix well. Continue cooking over medium heat for 3–4 minutes or until they are thoroughly warm.

Pour the tomato mixture over the tuna mixture and mix. Fold into the risotto 5 minutes before the end of the cooking time.

Remove the risotto from the heat when all the liquid has been absorbed and add the remaining butter. Mix well, then stir in the Parmesan until it melts. Serve at once.

bavettine with smoked salmon & arugula

ingredients

SERVES 4

12 oz/350 g dried bavettine

2 tbsp. olive oil

1 garlic clove, finely chopped

4 oz/115 g smoked salmon,
   cut into thin strips

2 oz/55 g arugula

salt and pepper

1/2 lemon, to garnish

method

Bring a large, heavy-bottom pan of lightly salted water to a boil. Add the pasta, return to a boil, and cook for 8–10 minutes, or until tender but still firm to the bite.

Just before the end of the cooking time, heat the olive oil in a heavy-bottom skillet. Add the garlic and cook over low heat, stirring constantly, for 1 minute. Do not allow the garlic to brown or it will taste bitter. Add the salmon and arugula. Season to taste with salt and pepper and cook, stirring constantly, for 1 minute. Remove the skillet from the heat.

Drain the pasta and transfer to a warmed serving dish. Add the smoked salmon and arugula mixture, toss lightly, and serve, garnished with a lemon half.

layered spaghetti with smoked salmon & shrimp

ingredients

SERVES 6

2¹/₂ oz/70 g butter, plus extra
for greasing

12 oz/350 g dried spaghetti

7 oz/200 g smoked salmon,
cut into strips

10 oz/280 g large jumbo
shrimp, cooked, shelled,
and deveined

1 quantity béchamel sauce
(see page 174)

4 oz/115 g/1 cup freshly
grated Parmesan cheese

salt

method

Butter a large, ovenproof dish and set aside.

Bring a large pan of lightly salted water to a boil. Add the pasta, bring back to a boil, and cook for 8–10 minutes, until tender but still firm to the bite. Drain well, return to the pan, add 2 oz/56 g of the butter, and toss well.

Spoon half the spaghetti into the prepared dish, cover with the strips of smoked salmon, then top with the shrimp. Pour over half the béchamel sauce and sprinkle with half the Parmesan. Add the remaining spaghetti, cover with the remaining sauce, and sprinkle with the remaining Parmesan. Dice the remaining butter and dot it over the surface.

Bake in a preheated oven, 350°F/180°C, for 15 minutes, until the top is golden. Serve immediately.

springtime pasta

ingredients

SERVES 4

2 tbsp. lemon juice

4 baby globe artichokes

7 tbsp. olive oil

2 shallots, chopped finely

2 garlic cloves, chopped finely

2 tbsp. chopped fresh flat-leaf
parsley

2 tbsp. chopped fresh mint

12 oz/350 g dried rigatoni or
other tubular pasta

12 large uncooked shrimp

1 oz/25 g unsalted butter

salt and pepper

method

Fill a bowl with cold water and add the lemon juice. Prepare the artichokes one at a time. Cut off the stems and trim away any tough outer leaves. Cut across the tops of the leaves. Slice in half lengthwise and remove the central fibrous chokes, then cut lengthwise into $1/4$-inch/0.75-cm thick slices. Place the slices in the bowl of acidulated water to prevent discoloration.

Heat 5 tablespoons of the olive oil in a heavy-bottom skillet. Drain the artichoke slices and pat dry with paper towels. Add them to the skillet with the shallots, garlic, parsley, and mint, and cook over low heat, stirring frequently, for 10–12 minutes until tender.

Meanwhile, bring a large pan of lightly salted water to a boil. Add the pasta, bring back to a boil, and cook for 8–10 minutes, until tender but still firm to the bite.

Shell the shrimp, cut a slit along the back of each, and remove and discard the dark vein. Melt the butter in a small skillet, cut the shrimp in half, and add them to the skillet. Cook, stirring occasionally, for 2–3 minutes, until they have changed color. Season to taste with salt and pepper.

Drain the pasta and pour it into a bowl. Add the remaining olive oil and toss well. Add the artichoke mixture and the shrimp and toss again. Serve immediately.

macaroni & seafood bake

ingredients

SERVES 4

12 oz/350 g dried
short-cut macaroni

6 tbsp. butter, plus extra for
greasing

2 small fennel bulbs,
thinly sliced

6 oz/175 g mushrooms, thinly
sliced

6 oz/175 g cooked
shelled shrimp

pinch of cayenne pepper

10 fl oz/300 ml/1 1/4 cups
béchamel sauce
(see page 174)

2 oz/55 g/1/2 cup freshly
grated parmesan cheese

2 large tomatoes, sliced

olive oil, for brushing

1 tsp. dried oregano

salt and pepper

method

Preheat the oven to 350°F/180°C. Bring a large pan of lightly salted water to a boil. Add the pasta, return to a boil, and cook for 8–10 minutes, or until tender but still firm to the bite. Drain and return to the pan. Add 2 tablespoons of the butter to the pasta, cover, shake the pan, and keep warm.

Melt the remaining butter in a separate pan. Add the fennel and cook for 3–4 minutes. Stir in the mushrooms and cook for an additional 2 minutes. Stir in the shrimp, then remove the pan from the heat. Stir the cayenne pepper into the béchamel sauce and add the shrimp mixture and pasta.

Grease a large ovenproof dish with butter, then pour the mixture into the dish and spread evenly. Sprinkle over the Parmesan cheese and arrange the tomato slices in a ring around the edge. Brush the tomatoes with olive oil, then sprinkle over the oregano. Bake in the preheated oven for 25 minutes, or until golden brown. Serve immediately.

shrimp & asparagus risotto

ingredients

SERVES 4

2 pints/1.2 litres/5 cups
    vegetable stock
12 oz/375 g fresh asparagus
    spears, cut into 2-inch/
    5-cm lengths
2 tbsp. olive oil
1 onion, finely chopped
1 garlic clove, finely chopped
12 oz/350 g/generous 1⅝
    cups risotto rice
1 lb/450 g raw jumbo shrimp,
    shelled and deveined
2 tbsp. olive paste or tapenade
2 tbsp. chopped fresh basil
salt and pepper
fresh Parmesan cheese
fresh basil sprigs, to garnish

method

Bring the stock to a boil in a large pan. Add the asparagus and cook for 3 minutes until just tender. Strain, reserving the stock, and refresh the asparagus under cold running water. Drain and set aside.

Return the stock to the pan and keep simmering gently over low heat while you are cooking the risotto.

Heat the olive oil in a large, heavy-bottom pan. Add the onion and cook over medium heat, stirring occasionally, for 5 minutes until softened. Add the garlic and cook for an additional 30 seconds.

Reduce the heat, add the rice, and mix to coat in oil. Cook, stirring constantly, for 2–3 minutes, or until the grains are translucent.

Gradually add the hot stock, a ladleful at a time. Stir constantly and add more liquid as the rice absorbs each addition. Increase the heat to medium so that the liquid bubbles. Cook for 20 minutes, until all the liquid is absorbed and the rice is creamy. Add the shrimp and asparagus with the last ladleful of stock.

Remove the pan from the heat, stir in the olive paste and basil, and season to taste with salt and pepper. Spoon the risotto onto warmed plates and serve at once, garnished with parmesan cheese and basil sprigs.

scallops with porcini & cream sauce

ingredients

SERVES 4

1 oz/25 g/1¹/₃ cups dried
    porcini mushrooms
18 fl oz/500 ml/generous
    2 cups hot water
3 tbsp. olive oil
3 tbsp. butter
12 oz/350 g/1¹/₂ cups
    scallops, sliced
2 garlic cloves, chopped
    very finely
2 tbsp. lemon juice
9 fl oz/250 ml/1 cup
    heavy cream
salt and pepper
12 oz/350 g dried fettuccine
    or pappardelle
2 tbsp. chopped fresh
    flat-leaf parsley,
    to serve

method

Put the porcini and hot water in a bowl. Let soak for 20 minutes. Strain the mushrooms, reserving the soaking water, and chop coarsely. Line a strainer with paper towels and strain the mushroom water into a bowl.

Heat the oil and butter in a large skillet over a medium heat. Add the scallops and cook for 2 minutes, or until just golden. Add the garlic and mushrooms, then stir-fry for another minute.

Stir in the lemon juice, cream, and 5 fl oz/150 ml/ ¹/₂ cup of the mushroom water. Bring to a boil, then simmer over a medium heat for 2–3 minutes, stirring constantly, until the liquid is reduced by half. Season with salt and pepper. Remove from the heat.

Cook the pasta in plenty of boiling salted water until al dente. Drain and transfer to a warm serving dish. Briefly reheat the sauce and pour over the pasta. Sprinkle with the parsley and toss well to mix. Serve immediately.

saffron & lemon risotto with scallops

ingredients

SERVES 4

2 pints/1.2 litres/5 cups
   simmering fish or
   vegetable stock
   (see page 76)
16 live scallops, shucked
juice of 1 lemon, plus extra
   for seasoning
1 tbsp. olive oil, plus extra
   for brushing
3 tbsp. butter
1 small onion, finely chopped
10 oz/280 g/generous
   1 3/8 cups risotto rice
1 tsp. crumbled saffron threads
2 tbsp. vegetable oil
4 oz/115 g/1 cup freshly
   grated parmesan or grana
   padano cheese
salt and pepper
1 lemon, cut into wedges
2 tsp. grated lemon zest,
   to garnish

method

Place the scallops in a nonmetallic bowl and mix with the lemon juice. Cover the bowl with plastic wrap and let chill in the refrigerator for 15 minutes.

Heat the oil with 2 tablespoons of the butter in a deep pan over medium heat until the butter has melted. Add the onion and cook, stirring, for 5 minutes, or until soft and starting to turn golden. Add the rice and mix to coat in oil and butter. Cook, stirring constantly, for 2–3 minutes, or until the grains are translucent. Dissolve the saffron in 4 tablespoons of hot stock and add to the rice.

Gradually add the remaining stock, a ladleful at a time. Stir constantly and add more liquid as the rice absorbs each addition. Increase the heat to medium so that the liquid bubbles. Cook for 20 minutes, or until all the liquid is absorbed and the rice is creamy. Season to taste.

When the risotto is nearly cooked, preheat a grill pan over high heat. Brush the scallops with oil and for 3–4 minutes on each side, depending on their thickness. Take care not to overcook or they will be rubbery.

Remove the risotto from the heat and add the remaining butter. Mix well, then stir in the Parmesan until it melts. Season with lemon juice, adding just 1 teaspoon at a time and tasting as you go.

Place a large scoop of risotto on each of 4 warmed plates. Arrange 4 scallops and lemon wedges around it, sprinkle with lemon zest, and serve at once.

risotto with squid & garlic butter

ingredients

SERVES 4

2 pints/1.2 litres/5 cups
   simmering fish or chicken
   stock (see page 76)
8–12 raw baby squid,
   cleaned, rinsed, and dried
5 1/2 oz/150 g butter
1 tbsp. olive oil
1 small onion, finely chopped
10 oz/280 g/generous
   1 3/8 cups risotto rice
3 garlic cloves, crushed
3 oz/85 g/3/4 cup freshly grated
   parmesan or grana padano
   cheese
salt and pepper
2 tbsp. finely chopped fresh
   parsley, to garnish

method

Dice the larger tentacles of the squid. Cut the squid in half lengthwise, then score with a sharp knife, making horizontal and vertical cuts.

Melt 2 tablespoons of the butter with the oil in a deep pan over medium heat. Stir in the onion and cook, stirring, for 5 minutes, or until soft and starting to turn golden. Add the rice and mix to coat in oil and butter. Cook, stirring constantly, for 2–3 minutes, or until the grains are translucent.

Gradually add the hot stock, a ladleful at a time. Stir constantly and add more liquid as the rice absorbs each addition. Increase the heat to medium so that the liquid bubbles. Cook for 20 minutes, or until all the liquid is absorbed and the rice is creamy. Season to taste.

When the risotto is nearly cooked, melt 4 oz/115 g of the remaining butter in a heavy-bottom skillet. Add the garlic and cook over low heat for 2 minutes, or until soft. Increase the heat to high, add the squid, and toss to cook. Do this for no more than 2–3 minutes or the squid will become tough. Remove the squid from the skillet, draining carefully and reserving the garlic butter.

Remove the risotto from the heat and add the remaining butter. Mix well, then stir in the Parmesan until it melts. Spoon the risotto onto warmed serving plates and arrange the squid on top. Spoon some of the garlic butter over each portion. Sprinkle with parsley and serve.

shellfish bake

ingredients

SERVES 6

12 oz/350 g dried conchiglie

6 tbsp. butter, plus extra
for greasing

2 fennel bulbs, thinly sliced

6 oz/175 g mushrooms,
thinly sliced

6 oz/175 g cooked
shelled shrimp

6 oz/175 g cooked crabmeat

pinch of cayenne pepper

10 fl oz/300 ml/1¼ cups
béchamel sauce
(see page 174)

2 oz/55 g/½ cup freshly
grated Parmesan cheese

2 beefsteak tomatoes, sliced

olive oil, for brushing

salt

to serve

green salad

crusty bread

method

Preheat the oven to 350°F/180°C. Bring a large, heavy-bottom pan of lightly salted water to a boil. Add the pasta, return to a boil, and cook for 8–10 minutes, or until tender but still firm to the bite. Drain well, return to the pan, and stir in 2 tablespoons of the butter. Cover the pan and keep warm.

Meanwhile, melt the remaining butter in a large, heavy-bottom skillet. Add the fennel and cook over medium heat for 5 minutes, or until softened. Stir in the mushrooms and cook for an additional 2 minutes. Stir in the shrimp and crabmeat, cook for an additional 1 minute, then remove the skillet from the heat.

Grease 6 small ovenproof dishes with butter. Stir the cayenne pepper into the béchamel sauce, add the shellfish mixture and pasta, then spoon into the prepared dishes. Sprinkle with the Parmesan cheese and arrange the tomato slices on top, then brush the tomatoes with a little olive oil.

Bake in the preheated oven for 25 minutes, or until golden brown. Serve hot with a green salad and crusty bread.

spaghetti with clams

ingredients

SERVES 4

2 lb 4 oz/1 kg live clams

6 fl oz/175 ml/3/4 cup water

6 fl oz/175 ml/3/4 cup dry
  white wine

12 oz/350 g dried spaghetti

5 tbsp. olive oil

2 garlic cloves, chopped finely

4 tbsp. chopped fresh flat-leaf
  parsley

salt and pepper

method

Scrub the clams under cold running water and discard any with broken or damaged shells or those that do not shut when sharply tapped. Place the clams in a large, heavy-bottom pan, add the water and wine, cover, and cook over high heat, shaking the pan occasionally, for 5 minutes, until the shells have opened.

Remove the clams with a slotted spoon and set aside to cool slightly. Strain the cooking liquid through a cheesecloth-lined strainer into a small pan. Bring to a boil and cook until reduced by about half and remove from heat. Meanwhile, discard any clams that have not opened, remove the remainder from their shells, and set aside.

Bring a large pan of lightly salted water to a boil. Add the pasta, bring back to a boil, and cook for 8–10 minutes, until tender but still firm to the bite.

Meanwhile, heat the olive oil in a large, heavy-bottom skillet. Add the garlic and cook, stirring frequently, for 2 minutes. Add the parsley and the reduced cooking liquid and let simmer gently.

Drain the pasta and add it to the skillet with the clams. Season to taste with salt and pepper and cook, stirring constantly, for 4 minutes, until the pasta is coated and the clams have heated through. Transfer to a warmed serving dish and serve immediately.

seafood pizza

ingredients

SERVES 2

1 quantity Pizza Dough
(see page 200)

all-purpose flour, for dusting

virgin olive oil, for drizzling

1 quantity Tomato Sauce
(see page 80)

8 oz/225 g mixed fresh
seafood, including cooked
shrimp, cooked mussels,
and squid rings

1/2 red bell pepper, seeded
and chopped

1/2 yellow bell pepper, seeded
and chopped

1 tbsp. capers, rinsed

2 oz/55 g Taleggio cheese,
grated

3 tbsp. freshly grated
Parmesan cheese

1/2 tsp. dried oregano

2³/4 oz/75 g anchovy fillets in
oil, drained and sliced

10 black olives, pitted

salt and pepper

method

Turn out the prepared pizza dough onto a lightly floured counter and knock down. Knead briefly, then roll out the dough into a circle about 1/4 inch/0.75 cm thick. Transfer to a lightly oiled baking sheet and push up the edge with your fingers to form a small rim.

Spread the tomato sauce over the pizza base, almost to the edge. Arrange the mixed seafood, red and yellow bell peppers, and capers evenly on top.

Sprinkle the Taleggio, Parmesan, and oregano evenly over the topping. Add the anchovy fillets and olives, drizzle with olive oil, and season to taste with salt and pepper.

Bake in a preheated oven, 425°F/220°C, for 20–25 minutes, until the crust is crisp and the cheese has melted. Serve immediately.

made with vegetables

Italian cuisine is ideal for those who like their food to center around vegetables cooked in interesting and innovative ways. It is a well-known fact that the Mediterranean diet is an exceptionally nutritious one, and this is largely because of the wide selection of intensely colored vegetables, including eggplants, tomatoes, zucchini, artichokes, and bell peppers, which combine with extra virgin olive oil to promote a healthy heart and tales of remarkable longevity.

This chapter has some warming and filling winter dishes, baked in the oven, as well as some light and delicious risotto recipes made vibrant in taste and color by glorious summer vegetables. A really good Parmesan cheese is the perfect ingredient to finish off a vegetable risotto (and indeed many Italian dishes) – by law, this most famous of Italian cheeses can be produced only in a tightly defined zone around Parma. Look for the words "Parmigiano Reggiano" and you will know that you have the real thing. Keep the cheese wrapped in aluminum foil in the refrigerator, and grate it freshly as required.

You will also find some mouthwatering pasta recipes in this chapter – pasta, again, lends itself to some excellent vegetable-based dishes, many of which are very quick and easy to prepare.

aubergines with mozzarella & parmesan

ingredients

SERVES 6–8

3 eggplants, sliced thinly

olive oil, for brushing

10 1/2 oz/300 g mozzarella di
    bufala, sliced

4 oz/115 g/1 cup freshly
    grated Parmesan cheese

3 tbsp. dried, uncolored
    bread crumbs

1 tbsp. butter

sprigs fresh flat-leaf parsley,
    to garnish

for the tomato and basil sauce

2 tbsp. virgin olive oil

4 shallots, chopped finely

2 garlic cloves, chopped
    finely

14 oz/400 g canned tomatoes

1 tsp. sugar

8 fresh basil leaves, shredded

salt and pepper

method

Arrange the eggplant slices in a single layer on one or two large baking sheets. Brush with olive oil and bake in a preheated oven, 400°F/200°C, for 15–20 minutes, until tender but not collapsing.

Meanwhile, make the tomato and basil sauce. Heat the oil in a heavy-bottom pan, add the shallots and cook, stirring occasionally, for 5 minutes, until softened. Add the garlic and cook for 1 minute more. Add the tomatoes, with their can juices, and break them up with a wooden spoon. Stir in the sugar, and season to taste with salt and pepper. Bring to a boil, reduce the heat, and let simmer for about 10 minutes, until thickened. Stir in the basil leaves.

Brush an ovenproof dish with olive oil and arrange half the eggplant slices in the bottom. Cover with half the mozzarella, spoon over half the tomato sauce, and sprinkle with half the Parmesan. Mix the remaining Parmesan with the bread crumbs. Make more layers, ending with the Parmesan mixture.

Dot the top with butter and bake for 25 minutes, until the topping is golden brown. Remove from the oven and let stand for 5 minutes, before slicing and serving, garnished with the parsley.

baked eggplant & tomatoes

ingredients

SERVES 4

1 lb 5 oz//600 g eggplant,
    cut into 1/2 -in/1-cm
    thick slices

salt

1 lb 5 oz/600 g plum
    tomatoes, cut into 1/2-in/
    1-cm thick slices

8 fl oz/225 ml/1 cup olive oil

salt and pepper

2 oz/5 g/1/2 cup freshly grated
    Parmesan cheese

2 tbsp. fresh white bread
    crumbs

method

To remove any bitterness, layer the eggplant slices in a colander, sprinkling each layer with salt. Stand the colander in the sink and let drain for 30 minutes. Meanwhile, spread out the tomato slices on paper towels, cover with more paper towels, and let drain.Rinse the eggplant thoroughly under cold running water to remove all traces of the salt, then pat dry with paper towels.

Heat 2 tablespoons of the olive oil in a large, heavy-bottom skillet. Add the tomato slices and cook for just 30 seconds on each side. Transfer to a large platter and season to taste with salt and pepper.

Wipe out the skillet with paper towels, then add 2 tablespoons of the remaining olive oil and heat. Add the eggplant slices, in batches, and cook on both sides until golden brown. Remove from the skillet and drain on paper towels. Cook the remaining slices in the same way, adding more olive oil as required.

Brush a large ovenproof dish with some of the remaining olive oil. Arrange alternate layers of eggplant and tomatoes, sprinkling each layer with Parmesan cheese. Top with the bread crumbs and drizzle with the remaining olive oil.

Bake in a preheated oven, 350°F/180°C, for 25–30 minutes, until golden. Serve immediately.

spinach & ricotta dumplings

ingredients

SERVES 4

2 lb 4 oz/1 kg fresh spinach,
coarse stalks removed

12 oz/350 g/1¹/₂ cups ricotta
cheese

4 oz/115 g/1 cup freshly
grated parmesan cheese

3 eggs, beaten lightly

pinch of freshly grated nutmeg

salt and pepper

4–6 oz/115–175 g/generous
³/₄ cup all-purpose flour,
plus extra for dusting

for the herb butter

4 oz/115 g unsalted butter

2 tbsp. chopped fresh oregano

2 tbsp. chopped fresh sage

method

Wash the spinach, then place it in a pan with just the water clinging to its leaves. Cover and cook over low heat for 6–8 minutes, until just wilted. Drain well and set aside to cool.

Squeeze or press out as much liquid as possible from the spinach, then chop finely. Place the spinach in a bowl and add the ricotta, half the Parmesan, the eggs, and nutmeg, and season to taste with salt and pepper. Beat until thoroughly combined. Start by sifting in 4 oz/ 115 g/ ³/₄ cup of the flour and lightly work it into the mixture, adding more, if necessary, to make a workable mixture. Cover with plastic wrap and let chill for 1 hour.

With floured hands, break off small pieces of the mixture and roll them into walnut-size balls. Handle them as little as possible, because they are quite delicate. Lightly dust the dumplings with flour.

Bring a large pan of lightly salted water to a boil. Add the dumplings and cook for 2–3 minutes, until they rise to the surface. Remove them from the pan with a slotted spoon, drain well, and set aside.

Meanwhile, make the herb butter. Melt the butter in a large, heavy-bottom skillet. Add the oregano and sage and cook over low heat, stirring frequently, for 1 minute. Add the dumplings and toss gently for 1 minute to coat. Transfer to a warmed serving dish, sprinkle with the remaining Parmesan, and serve.

spinach & ricotta ravioli

ingredients

SERVES 4

12 oz/350 g fresh spinach
leaves, coarse stalks
removed
8 oz/225 g/1 cup ricotta
cheese
2 oz/55 g/¹/₂ cup freshly
grated Parmesan cheese
2 eggs, lightly beaten
pinch of freshly grated nutmeg
pepper
all-purpose flour, for dusting
freshly grated Parmesan
cheese, to serve (optional)

spinach pasta dough

1¹/₃ cups white all-purpose
flour, plus extra for dusting
pinch of salt
8 oz/225 g frozen spinach,
thawed, squeezed dry,
and finely chopped
2 eggs, lightly beaten
1 tbsp olive oil

method

To make the pasta dough, sift the flour into a food processor and add the salt. Add the chopped spinach, then pour in the eggs and olive oil and process until the dough begins to come together. Turn out onto a lightly floured counter and knead until smooth. Wrap in plastic wrap and let rest for at least 30 minutes.

Cook the spinach, with just the water clinging to the leaves after washing, over low heat for 5 minutes until wilted. Drain and squeeze out as much moisture as possible. Cool, then chop finely. Beat the ricotta cheese until smooth, then stir in the spinach, Parmesan, and half the egg and season to taste with nutmeg and pepper.

Halve the pasta dough. Cover one piece and thinly roll out the other on a floured counter. Cover and roll out the second piece. Put small mounds of filling in rows 1¹/₂ inches/4 cm apart on one sheet of dough and brush the spaces in between with the remaining beaten egg. Lift the second piece of dough to fit on top. Press down between the mounds, pushing out any air. Cut into squares and rest on a dish towel for 1 hour.

Bring a large pan of salted water to a boil, add the ravioli, in batches, return to a boil, and cook for 5 minutes. Remove with a slotted spoon and drain on paper towels. Serve with grated Parmesan cheese, if liked.

radiatori with pumpkin sauce

ingredients

SERVES 4

for the sauce

2 oz/55 g unsalted butter

4 oz/115 g white onions
  or shallots, chopped
  very finely

salt

1 lb 12 oz/800 g pumpkin,
  unprepared weight

pinch of freshly grated
  nutmeg

12 oz/350 g dried radiatori

7 fl oz/200 ml/scant 1 cup
  light cream

4 tbsp. freshly grated
  parmesan cheese,
  plus extra to serve

2 tbsp. chopped fresh flat-leaf
  parsley

salt and pepper

method

Melt the butter in a heavy-bottom pan over low heat. Add the onions, sprinkle with a little salt, cover, and cook, stirring frequently, for 25–30 minutes.

Scoop out and discard the seeds from the pumpkin. Peel and finely chop the flesh. Add the pumpkin to the pan and season to taste with nutmeg. Cover and cook over low heat, stirring occasionally, for 45 minutes.

Meanwhile, bring a large pan of lightly salted water to a boil. Add the pasta, bring back to a boil, and cook for 8–10 minutes, until tender but still firm to the bite. Drain thoroughly, reserving about $1/4$ pint/150 ml/ $2/3$ cup of the cooking liquid.

Stir the cream, grated Parmesan, and parsley into the pumpkin sauce and season to taste with salt and pepper. If the mixture seems a little too thick, add some or all of the reserved cooking liquid. Pour in the pasta and toss for 1 minute. Serve immediately, with extra parmesan for sprinkling.

vegetarian lasagna

ingredients

SERVES 4

olive oil, for brushing

2 eggplants, sliced

2 tbsp. butter

1 garlic clove, finely chopped

4 zucchini, sliced

1 tbsp. finely chopped fresh
flat-leaf parsley

1 tbsp. finely chopped fresh
marjoram

8 oz/225 g mozzarella
cheese, grated

1 pint/600 ml/2½ cups
strained canned tomatoes

175 g/6 oz dried no-precook
lasagna

salt and pepper

1 pint/600 ml/2½ cups
béchamel sauce
(see page 174)

2 oz/55 g/½ cup freshly
grated parmesan cheese

method

Preheat the oven to 400°F/200°C. Brush a large ovenproof dish with olive oil. Brush a large grill pan with olive oil and heat until smoking. Add half the eggplant slices and cook over medium heat for 8 minutes, or until golden brown all over. Remove the eggplant from the grill pan and drain on paper towels. Add the remaining eggplant slices and extra oil, if necessary, and cook for 8 minutes, or until golden brown all over.

Melt the butter in a skillet and add the garlic, zucchini, parsley, and marjoram. Cook over medium heat, stirring frequently, for 5 minutes, or until the zucchini are golden brown all over. Remove from the skillet and let drain on paper towels.

Layer the eggplant, zucchini, mozzarella, strained tomatoes, and lasagna in the dish, seasoning with salt and pepper as you go and finishing with a layer of lasagna. Pour over the béchamel sauce, making sure that all the pasta is covered. Sprinkle with the grated Parmesan cheese and bake in the preheated oven for 30–40 minutes, or until golden brown. Serve the lasagna immediately.

mixed vegetable agnolotti

ingredients

SERVES 4

butter, for greasing
1 quantity basic pasta dough
all-purpose flour, for dusting
3 oz/85 g/3/4 cup freshly
    grated parmesan cheese
mixed salad greens, to serve

filling

4 fl oz/125 ml/1/2 cup olive oil
1 red onion, chopped
3 garlic cloves, chopped
2 large eggplants,
    cut into chunks
3 large zucchini, cut into
    chunks
6 beefsteak tomatoes,
    peeled, seeded, and
    coarsely chopped
1 large green bell pepper,
    seeded and diced
1 large red bell pepper,
    seeded and diced
1 tbsp. sun-dried tomato paste
1 tbsp. shredded fresh basil
salt and pepper

method

Preheat the oven to 400°F/200°C. To make the filling, heat the olive oil in a large, heavy-bottom pan. Add the onion and garlic and cook over low heat, stirring occasionally, for 5 minutes, or until softened. Add the eggplant, zucchini, tomatoes, green and red bell peppers, sun-dried tomato paste, and basil. Season to taste with salt and pepper, cover, and let simmer gently, stirring occasionally, for 20 minutes.

Lightly grease an ovenproof dish with butter. Roll out the pasta dough on a lightly floured counter and stamp out 3-inch/7.5-cm circles with a plain cutter. Place a spoonful of the vegetable filling on one side of each circle. Dampen the edges slightly and fold the pasta circles over, pressing together to seal.

Bring a large pan of lightly salted water to a boil. Add the agnolotti, in batches if necessary, return to a boil, and cook for 3–4 minutes. Remove with a slotted spoon, drain, and transfer to the dish. Sprinkle with the Parmesan cheese and bake in the preheated oven for 20 minutes. Serve with salad greens.

penne in a creamy mushroom sauce

ingredients

SERVES 4

4 tbsp. butter

1 tbsp. olive oil

6 shallots, sliced

1 lb/450 g cremini mushrooms,
    sliced

salt and pepper

1 tsp. all-purpose flour

5 fl oz/150 ml/$2/3$ cup heavy
    cream or panna da cucina

2 tbsp. port

4 oz/115 g sun-dried
    tomatoes in oil, drained
    and chopped

pinch of freshly grated nutmeg

12 oz/350 g dried penne

2 tbsp. chopped fresh
    flat-leaf parsley

method

Melt the butter with the olive oil in a large heavy-bottom skillet. Add the shallots and cook over low heat, stirring occasionally, for 4–5 minutes, or until softened. Add the mushrooms and cook over low heat for an additional 2 minutes. Season to taste with salt and pepper, sprinkle in the flour and cook, stirring, for 1 minute.

Remove the skillet from the heat and gradually stir in the cream and port. Return to the heat, add the sun-dried tomatoes, and grated nutmeg, and cook over low heat, stirring occasionally, for 8 minutes.

Meanwhile, bring a large heavy-bottom pan of lightly salted water to a boil. Add the pasta, return to a boil, and cook for 8–10 minutes, or until tender but still firm to the bite. Drain the pasta well and add to the mushroom sauce. Cook for 3 minutes, then transfer to a warmed serving dish. Sprinkle with the chopped parsley and serve immediately.

baked pasta with mushrooms

ingredients

SERVES 4

5 oz/140 g fontina cheese, sliced thinly

3 oz/85 g butter, plus extra for greasing

12 oz/350 g mixed exotic mushrooms, sliced

12 oz/350 g dried tagliatelle

2 egg yolks

salt and pepper

4 tbsp. freshly grated pecorino cheese

for the béchamel sauce

2 oz/55 g unsalted butter

2 oz/55 g/3/8 cup all-purpose flour

18 fl oz/500 ml/generous 2 cups milk

1 bay leaf

salt and pepper

pinch of freshly grated nutmeg

method

To make the béchamel sauce, melt the butter, add the flour, and cook over low heat, stirring constantly, for 1 minute. Remove the pan from the heat and gradually stir in the milk. Return the pan to the heat and bring to a boil, stirring constantly, until thickened and smooth. Add the bay leaf and let simmer gently for 2 minutes. Remove the bay leaf and season the sauce to taste with salt, pepper, and nutmeg. Remove the pan from the heat. Stir in the fontina cheese and set aside.

Melt 1 oz/28 g of the butter in a large pan. Add the mushrooms and cook over low heat, stirring occasionally, for 10 minutes.

Meanwhile, bring a large pan of lightly salted water to a boil. Add the pasta, bring back to a boil, and cook for 8–10 minutes, until tender but still firm to the bite. Drain, return to the pan, and add the remaining butter, the egg yolks, and about one-third of the béchamel sauce, then season to taste with salt and pepper. Toss well to mix, then gently stir in the mushrooms.

Lightly grease a large, ovenproof dish and spoon in the pasta mixture. Pour over the remaining sauce evenly and sprinkle with the grated pecorino. Bake in a preheated oven, 400°F/200°C, for 15–20 minutes, until golden brown. Serve immediately.

mushroom cannelloni

ingredients

SERVES 4

2 dried cannelloni tubes

4 tbsp. olive oil, plus extra
   for brushing

2 tbsp. butter

1 lb/450 g mixed wild
   mushrooms, finely chopped

1 garlic clove, finely chopped

3 oz/85 g/1 1/2 cups fresh
   bread crumbs

5 fl oz/150 ml/2/3 cup milk

8 oz/225 g/1 cup ricotta
   cheese

6 tbsp. freshly grated
   parmesan cheese

2 tbsp. pine nuts

2 tbsp. slivered almonds

salt and pepper

tomato sauce

2 tbsp. olive oil

1 onion, finely chopped

1 garlic clove, finely chopped

1 lb 12 oz/800 g canned
   chopped tomatoes

1 tbsp. tomato paste

8 pitted black olives, chopped

salt and pepper

method

Preheat the oven to 375°F/190°C. Bring a large pan of lightly salted water to a boil. Add the cannelloni tubes, return to a boil, and cook for 8–10 minutes, or until tender but still firm to the bite. With a slotted spoon, transfer the cannelloni tubes to a plate and pat dry. Brush a large ovenproof dish with olive oil.

Meanwhile, make the tomato sauce. Heat the olive oil in a skillet. Add the onion and garlic and cook over low heat for 5 minutes, or until softened. Add the tomatoes and their can juices, tomato paste, and olives and season to taste with salt and pepper. Bring to a boil and cook for 3–4 minutes. Pour the sauce into the ovenproof dish.

To make the filling, melt the butter in a heavy-bottom skillet. Add the mushrooms and garlic and cook over medium heat, stirring frequently, for 3–5 minutes, or until tender. Remove the skillet from the heat. Mix the bread crumbs, milk, and olive oil together in a large bowl, then stir in the ricotta, mushroom mixture, and 4 tablespoons of the Parmesan cheese. Season to taste with salt and pepper.

Fill the cannelloni tubes with the mushroom mixture and place them in the dish. Brush with olive oil and sprinkle with the remaining Parmesan cheese, pine nuts, and almonds. Bake in the oven for 25 minutes, or until golden.

fusilli with gorgonzola & mushroom sauce

ingredients

SERVES 4

12 oz/350 g dried fusilli

3 tbsp. olive oil

12 oz/350 g exotic
   mushrooms, sliced

1 garlic clove, chopped finely

14 fl oz/400 ml/1¾ cups
   heavy cream

9 oz/250 g gorgonzola
   cheese, crumbled

salt and pepper

2 tbsp. chopped fresh flat-leaf
   parsley, to garnish

method

Bring a large pan of lightly salted water to a boil. Add the pasta, bring back to a boil, and cook for 8–10 minutes, until tender but still firm to the bite.

Meanwhile, heat the olive oil in a heavy-bottom pan. Add the mushrooms and cook over low heat, stirring frequently, for 5 minutes. Add the garlic and cook for an additional 2 minutes.

Add the cream, bring to a boil, and cook for 1 minute, until slightly thickened. Stir in the cheese and cook over low heat until it has melted. Do not let the sauce boil once the cheese has been added. Season to taste with salt and pepper and remove the pan from the heat.

Drain the pasta and pour it into the sauce. Toss well to coat, then serve immediately, garnished with the parsley.

penne with pepper & goat cheese sauce

ingredients

SERVES 4

2 tbsp. olive oil

1 tbsp. butter

1 small onion, chopped finely

4 bell peppers, yellow and
   red, seeded and cut into
   3/4 inch/2 cm squares

3 garlic cloves, sliced thinly

salt and pepper

1 lb/450 g/4 cups dried
   rigatoni or penne

4¹/₂ oz/125 g goat cheese,
   crumbled

15 fresh basil leaves, shredded

10 black olives, pitted and
   sliced

method

Heat the oil and butter in a large skillet over a medium heat. Add the onion and cook until soft. Raise the heat to medium–high and add the bell peppers and garlic. Cook for 12–15 minutes, stirring, until the peppers are tender but not mushy. Season with salt and pepper. Remove from the heat.

Cook the pasta in plenty of boiling salted water until al dente. Drain and transfer to a warm serving dish. Add the goat cheese and toss to mix.

Briefly reheat the sauce. Add the basil and olives. Pour over the pasta and toss well to mix. Serve immediately.

spaghetti with roasted garlic & pepper sauce

ingredients

SERVES 4

6 large garlic cloves,
   unpeeled

14 oz/400 g bottled roasted
   red bell peppers, drained
   and sliced

7 oz/200 g canned chopped
   tomatoes

3 tbsp. olive oil

1/4 tsp. dried chili flakes

1 tsp. chopped fresh thyme
   or oregano

salt and pepper

12 oz/350 g dried spaghetti,
   bucatini, or linguine

freshly grated Parmesan,
   to serve

method

Place the unpeeled garlic cloves in a shallow, ovenproof dish. Roast in a preheated oven at 400°F/200°C for 7–10 minutes, or until the cloves feel soft.

Put the bell peppers, tomatoes, and oil in a food processor or blender, then purée. Squeeze the garlic flesh into the purée. Add the chili flakes and oregano. Season with salt and pepper. Blend again, then scrape into a pan and set aside.

Cook the pasta in plenty of boiling salted water until al dente. Drain and transfer to a warm serving dish.

Reheat the sauce and pour over the pasta. Toss well to mix. Serve at once with parmesan.

hot chili pasta

ingredients

SERVES 4

$^1/_4$ pint/150 ml/$^2/_3$ cup dry
   white wine
1 tbsp. sun-dried
   tomato paste
2 fresh red chilies
2 garlic cloves,
   finely chopped
12 oz/350 g dried tortiglioni
4 tbsp. chopped fresh
   flat-leaf parsley
salt and pepper
fresh romano cheese
   shavings, to garnish

for the sugocasa

5 tbsp. extra-virgin olive oil
1 lb/450 g plum tomatoes,
   chopped
salt and pepper

method

First make the sugocasa. Heat the olive oil in a skillet until it is almost smoking. Add the tomatoes and cook over high heat for 2–3 minutes. Reduce the heat to low and cook gently for 20 minutes, or until very soft. Season with salt and pepper, then pass through a food mill or blender into a clean pan.

Add the wine, sun-dried tomato paste, whole chilies, and garlic to the sugocasa and bring to a boil. Reduce the heat and simmer gently.

Meanwhile, bring a large pan of lightly salted water to a boil. Add the pasta, return to a boil, and cook for 8–10 minutes, or until tender but still firm to the bite.

Meanwhile, remove the chilies and taste the sauce. If you prefer a hotter flavor, chop some or all of the chilies and return them to the pan. Check the seasoning at the same time, then stir in half the parsley.

Drain the pasta and tip it into a warmed serving bowl. Add the sauce and toss to coat. Sprinkle with the remaining parsley, garnish with the romano shavings, and serve immediately.

minted green risotto

ingredients

SERVES 6

1³/₄ pints/1 litre/4 cups
simmering chicken or
vegetable stock
(see page 76)

2 tbsp. butter

8 oz/225 g/generous 1¹/₂ cups
shelled fresh peas or
thawed frozen peas

9 oz/250 g/5⁵/₈ cups fresh
young spinach leaves,
washed and drained

1 bunch of fresh mint, leaves
stripped from stalks

2 tbsp. chopped fresh basil

2 tbsp. chopped fresh oregano

pinch of freshly grated nutmeg

4 tbsp. mascarpone cheese
or heavy cream

2 tbsp. vegetable oil

1 onion, finely chopped

2 celery stalks, including
leaves, finely chopped

2 garlic cloves, finely chopped

¹/₂ tsp. dried thyme

10¹/₂ oz/300 g/ scant 1¹/₂
cups risotto rice

2 fl oz/50 ml/¹/₄ cup dry white
vermouth

3 oz/85 g/³/₄ cup freshly
grated parmesan cheese

method

Heat half the butter in a deep skillet over medium-high heat until sizzling. Add the peas, spinach, mint leaves, basil, and oregano and season with the nutmeg. Cook, stirring frequently, for 3 minutes, or until the spinach and mint leaves are wilted. Let cool slightly.

Pour the spinach mixture into a food processor and process for 15 seconds. Add the mascarpone (or cream) and process again for 1 minute. Transfer to a bowl and set aside.

Heat the oil and remaining butter in a large, heavy-bottom pan over medium heat. Add the onion, celery, garlic, and thyme and cook, stirring occasionally, for 2 minutes, or until the vegetables are softened.

Reduce the heat, add the rice, and mix to coat in oil and butter. Cook, stirring constantly, for 2–3 minutes, or until the grains are translucent.

Add the vermouth and cook, stirring constantly, until it has reduced.

Gradually add the hot stock, a ladleful at a time. Stir constantly and add more liquid as the rice absorbs each addition. Increase the heat to medium so that the liquid bubbles. Cook for 20 minutes, or until the liquid is absorbed and the rice is creamy.

Stir in the spinach-mascarpone mixture and the Parmesan. Transfer to warmed plates and serve at once.

risotto with roasted vegetables

ingredients

SERVES 4

2 pints/1.2 litres/5 cups
   simmering chicken or
   vegetable stock
   (see page 76)
1 tbsp. olive oil
3 tbsp. butter
1 small onion, finely chopped
10 oz/280 g/generous 1³/₈
   cups risotto rice
8 oz/225 g roasted vegetables,
   such as bell peppers,
   zucchini, and eggplant,
   cut into chunks
3 oz/85 g/³/₄ cup freshly grated
   parmesan or grana padano
   cheese
salt and pepper
2 tbsp. finely chopped fresh
   herbs, to garnish

method

Heat the oil with 2 tablespoons of the butter in a deep pan over medium heat until the butter has melted. Add the onion and cook, stirring occasionally, for 5 minutes, until soft and starting to turn golden. Do not brown.

Reduce the heat, add the rice, and mix to coat in oil and butter. Cook, stirring constantly, for 2–3 minutes, or until the grains are translucent.

Gradually add the hot stock, a ladleful at a time. Stir constantly and add more liquid as the rice absorbs each addition. Increase the heat to medium so that the liquid bubbles. Cook for 15 minutes, then add most of the roasted vegetables, setting aside a few pieces to use as a garnish. Cook for an additional 5 minutes, or until all the liquid is absorbed and the rice is creamy. Season to taste with salt and pepper.

Remove the risotto from the heat and add the remaining butter. Mix well, then stir in the Parmesan until it melts. Spoon the risotto onto warmed individual plates, arrange vegetables around it or on top to garnish, and then sprinkle with fresh herbs before serving at once.

risotto with artichoke hearts

ingredients

SERVES 4

2 pints/1.2 litres/5 cups
  simmering chicken or
  vegetable stock
  (see page 76)
8 oz/225 g canned artichoke
  hearts
1 tbsp. olive oil
3 tbsp. butter
1 small onion, finely chopped
g0 oz/280 g/generous 1³/₈
  cups risotto rice
3 oz/85 g/³/₄ cup freshly grated
  parmesan or grana padano
  cheese
salt and pepper
fresh flat-leaf parsley sprigs,
  to garnish

method

Drain the artichoke hearts, reserving the liquid, and cut them into fourths.

Heat the oil with 2 tablespoons of the butter in a deep pan over medium heat until the butter has melted. Stir in the onion and cook gently, stirring occasionally, for 5 minutes, or until soft and starting to turn golden. Do not brown.

Add the rice and mix to coat in oil and butter. Cook, stirring constantly, for 2–3 minutes, or until the grains are translucent.

Gradually add the artichoke liquid and the hot stock, a ladle at a time. Stir constantly and add more liquid as the rice absorbs each addition. Increase the heat to medium so that the liquid bubbles. Cook for 15 minutes, then add the artichoke hearts. Cook for an additional 5 minutes, or until all the liquid is absorbed and the rice is creamy. Season to taste.

Remove the risotto from the heat and add the remaining butter. Mix well, then stir in the Parmesan until it melts. Season, if necessary. Spoon the risotto into warmed bowls, garnish with parsley sprigs, and serve at once.

asparagus & sun-dried tomato risotto

ingredients

SERVES 4

1³/₄ pints/1 litre/4 cups
    simmering vegetable stock
    (see page 76)
1 tbsp. olive oil
3 tbsp. butter
1 small onion, finely chopped
6 sun-dried tomatoes, thinly
    sliced
10 oz/280 g/generous
    1³/₈ cups risotto rice
5 fl oz/150 ml/²/₃ cup dry
    white wine
8 oz/225 g fresh asparagus
    spears, cooked
3 oz/85 g/³/₄ cup freshly
    grated parmesan or grana
    padano cheese
salt and pepper
thinly pared lemon rind,
    to garnish

method

Heat the oil with 2 tablespoons of the butter in a deep pan over medium heat until the butter has melted. Stir in the onion and sun-dried tomatoes, and cook, stirring occasionally, for 5 minutes until the onion is soft and starting to turn golden. Do not brown.

Reduce the heat, add the rice, and mix to coat in oil and butter. Cook, stirring constantly, for 2–3 minutes, or until the grains are translucent.

Add the wine and cook, stirring constantly, until it has reduced. Gradually add the hot stock, a ladleful at a time. Stir constantly and add more liquid as the rice absorbs each addition. Increase the heat to medium so that the liquid bubbles. Cook for 20 minutes, or until all the liquid is absorbed and the rice is creamy. Season to taste.

While the risotto is cooking, cut most of the asparagus into pieces about 1 inch/2.5 cm long. Keep several spears whole for garnishing the finished dish. Carefully fold the cut pieces of asparagus into the risotto for the last 5 minutes of cooking time.

Remove the risotto from the heat and add the remaining butter. Mix well, then stir in the Parmesan until it melts. Spoon the risotto onto individual warmed serving dishes and garnish with whole spears of asparagus. Sprinkle the lemon rind on top and serve.

risotto primavera

ingredients

SERVES 6–8

2³/4 pints/1.5 litres/generous
6 1/3 cups simmering
chicken or vegetable stock
(see page 76)

8 oz/225 g fresh thin
asparagus spears

4 tbsp. olive oil

6 oz/175 g young green beans,
cut into 1-inch/2.5-cm
lengths

6 oz/175 g young zucchini,
quartered and cut into
1-inch/2.5-cm lengths

8 oz/225 g/generous 1¹/2
cups shelled fresh peas

1 onion, finely chopped

1–2 garlic cloves, finely
chopped

12 oz/350 g/generous
1⁵/8 cups risotto rice

4 scallions, cut into
1-inch/2.5-cm lengths

2 oz/55 g butter

4 oz/115 g/1 cup freshly
grated Parmesan cheese

2 tbsp. snipped fresh chives

2 tbsp. shredded fresh basil

salt and pepper

scallions, to garnish (optional)

method

Trim the woody ends of the asparagus and cut off the tips. Cut the stems into 1-inch/2.5-cm pieces and set aside with the tips.

Heat 2 tablespoons of the oil in a large skillet over high heat until very hot. Add the asparagus, beans, zucchini, and peas and stir-fry for 3–4 minutes until they are bright green and just starting to soften. Set aside.

Heat the remaining oil in a large, heavy-bottom pan over medium heat. Add the onion and cook, stirring occasionally, for 3 minutes, or until it starts to soften. Stir in the garlic and cook, while stirring, for 30 seconds. Reduce the heat, add the rice, and mix to coat in oil. Cook, stirring constantly, for 2–3 minutes, or until the grains are translucent.

Gradually add the hot stock, a ladleful at a time. Stir constantly and add more liquid as the rice absorbs each addition. Increase the heat to medium so that the liquid bubbles. Cook for 20 minutes, or until all but 2 tablespoons of the liquid is absorbed and the rice is creamy.

Stir in the stir-fried vegetables, onion mixture, and scallions with the remaining stock. Cook for 2 minutes, stirring frequently, then season to taste with salt and pepper. Stir in the butter, Parmesan, chives, and basil.

Remove the pan from the heat. Transfer the risotto to a warmed serving dish, garnish with scallions, if liked, and serve at once.

wild mushroom risotto

ingredients

SERVES 6

2 pints/1/2 litres/5 cups
simmering chicken or
vegetable stock
(see page 76)

2 oz/55 g/1/2 cup dried porcini
or morel mushrooms

about 1 lb 2 oz/500 g mixed
fresh wild mushrooms,
such as porcini, horse
mushrooms, and
chanterelles, halved
if large

4 tbsp. olive oil

3–4 garlic cloves, finely chopped

2 oz/55 g butter

1 onion, finely chopped

12 oz/350 g/generous 1⁵/₈
cups risotto rice

2 fl oz/50 ml/1/4 cup dry
white vermouth

4 oz/115 g/1 cup freshly
grated Parmesan cheese

4 tbsp. chopped fresh
flat-leaf parsley

salt and pepper

method

Place the dried mushrooms in a heatproof bowl and add boiling water to cover. Set aside to soak for 30 minutes, then carefully lift out and pat dry. Strain the soaking liquid through a strainer lined with paper towels and set aside.

Trim the fresh mushrooms and gently brush clean. Heat 3 tablespoons of the oil in a large skillet. Add the fresh mushrooms and stir-fry for 1–2 minutes. Add the garlic and the soaked mushrooms and cook, stirring frequently, for 2 minutes. Transfer to a plate.

Heat the remaining oil and half the butter in a large, heavy-bottom pan. Add the onion and cook over medium heat, stirring occasionally, for 2 minutes, until softened.

Reduce the heat, add the rice, and mix to coat in oil and butter. Cook, stirring constantly, for 2–3 minutes, or until the grains are translucent.

Add the vermouth and cook, stirring constantly, for 1 minute until reduced.

Gradually add the hot stock, a ladleful at a time. Stir constantly and add more liquid as the rice absorbs each addition. Increase the heat to medium so that the liquid bubbles. Cook for 20 minutes, or until all the liquid is absorbed and the rice is creamy.

Add half the reserved mushroom soaking liquid to the risotto and stir in the mushrooms. Season to taste with salt and pepper and add more mushroom liquid, if necessary. Remove the pan from the heat and stir in the remaining butter, the grated Parmesan, and chopped parsley. Serve at once.

risotto with four cheeses

ingredients

SERVES 6

1³/₄ pints/1 litre/4 cups
  simmering vegetable stock
  (see page 76)
1¹/₂ oz/ 40 g/ unsalted butter
1 onion, chopped finely
12 oz/350 g/generous 1¹/₂
  cups risotto rice
7 fl oz/200 ml/scant 1 cup dry
  white wine
2 oz/55 g/¹/₂ cup Gorgonzola
  cheese, crumbled
2 oz/55 g/¹/₂ cup freshly
  grated taleggio cheese
2 oz/55 g/¹/₂ cup freshly
  grated fontina cheese
2 oz/55 g/¹/₂ cup freshly
  grated parmesan cheese
salt and pepper
2 tbsp. chopped fresh flat-leaf
  parsley, to garnish

method

Melt the butter in another large, heavy-bottom pan. Add the onion and cook over low heat, stirring occasionally, for 5 minutes, until softened. Add the rice and cook, stirring constantly, for 2–3 minutes, until all the grains are thoroughly coated and glistening.

Add the wine and cook, stirring constantly, until it has almost completely evaporated. Add a ladleful of the hot stock and cook, stirring constantly, until all the stock has been absorbed. Continue cooking, stirring and adding the stock, a ladleful at a time, for about 20 minutes, or until the rice is tender and the liquid has been absorbed.

Remove the pan from the heat and stir in the Gorgonzola, Taleggio, fontina, and about one-quarter of the Parmesan until melted. Season to taste with salt and pepper. Transfer the risotto to a warmed serving dish, sprinkle with the remaining Parmesan, garnish with the parsley, and serve immediately.

cheese & tomato pizza

ingredients

SERVES 2

for the dough

8 oz/225 g/1 1/2 cups all-
  purpose flour, plus extra
  for dusting
1 tsp. salt
1 tsp. active dry yeast
1 tbsp. olive oil, plus extra for
  brushing
6 tbsp. lukewarm water

for the topping

6 tomatoes, sliced thinly
6 oz/175 g/mozzarella
  cheese, drained and
  sliced thinly
salt and pepper
2 tbsp. shredded fresh basil
  leaves
2 tbsp. olive oil

method

To make the pizza dough, sift the flour and salt into a bowl and stir in the yeast. Make a well in the center and pour in the oil and water. Gradually incorporate the dry ingredients into the liquid, using a wooden spoon or floured hands.

Turn out the dough onto a lightly floured counter and knead well for 5 minutes, until smooth and elastic. Return to the clean bowl, covered with lightly oiled plastic wrap, and set aside to rise in a warm place for about 1 hour, or until doubled in size.

Turn out the dough onto a lightly floured counter and knock down. Knead briefly, then cut it in half and roll out each piece into a circle about 1/4 inch/0.75 cm thick. Transfer to a lightly oiled baking sheet and push up the edges with your fingers to form a small rim.

For the topping, arrange the tomato and mozzarella slices alternately over the pizza bases. Season to taste with salt and pepper, sprinkle with the basil, and drizzle with the olive oil.

Bake in a preheated oven, 450°F/230°C, for 15–20 minutes, until the crust is crisp and the cheese has melted. Serve immediately.

to finish

Everyday Italian meals usually finish with fresh fruit, or perhaps a choice of cheese, but when it comes to a special occasion, the Italians know how to come up with something that is as stylish as it is delicious. Usually they will head to the local *pasticceria* for an elaborate confection, or perhaps to the *gelateria* for some of the mouthwatering ice creams for which Italy is famous.

However, there are plenty of Italian desserts that can be made at home, and this chapter has a selection of the best. Many of the most delicious desserts come from southern Italy and from the islands of Sicily and Sardinia, where fruit, nuts, and honey are key ingredients. Wines, liqueurs, and spirits also make a frequent appearance, especially Amaretto, a distinctive almond-flavored liqueur, and the delectably rich, sweet, Marsala wine that goes into *zabaglione*, a superb dessert that takes courage as well as skill to create as it must be cooked then served immediately!

One Italian dessert that was "invented" in the 1970s, and has since reached almost cult status, is *tiramisù*, a wonderful combination of sponge cake soaked in a mixture of rum and black coffee layered with sweetened mascarpone, the delicately flavored cream cheese used in both sweet and savory dishes.

chocolate & amaretto cheesecake

ingredients

SERVES 10–12

oil, for brushing
6 oz/175 g graham crackers
2 oz/55 g amaretti cookies
3 oz/85 g butter

filling

8 oz/225 g semisweet
    chocolate
14 oz/400 g/1³/₄ cups
    cream cheese
4 oz/115 g/generous ¹/₂ cup
    golden superfine sugar
3 tbsp. all-purpose flour
1 tsp. vanilla extract
4 eggs
10 fl oz/300 ml/1¹/₄ cups
    heavy cream
2 fl oz/50 ml/¹/₄ cup amaretto
    liqueur

topping

1 tbsp. amaretto liqueur
³/₄ cup crème fraîche
crushed amaretti cookies

method

Line the bottom of a 9-inch/23-cm springform cake pan with foil and brush the sides with oil. Place the graham crackers and amaretti cookies in a plastic bag and crush with a rolling pin. Place the butter in a pan and heat until just melted, then stir in the crushed cookies. Press the mixture into the bottom of the pan and let chill for 1 hour.

Preheat the oven to 325°F/160°C. To make the filling, melt the chocolate in a small heatproof bowl over a saucepan of gently simmering water, then let cool. Place the cream cheese in a bowl and beat until fluffy, then add the sugar, flour, and vanilla extract and beat together until smooth. Gradually add the eggs, beating until well blended. Blend in the melted chocolate, cream, and amaretto liqueur. Pour the mixture over the chilled biscuit base and bake in the oven for 50–60 minutes, or until set.

Leave the cheesecake in the oven with the door slightly ajar, until cold. Run a knife round the inside of the pan to loosen the cheesecake. Let chill in the refrigerator for 2 hours, then remove from the pan and place on a serving plate. To make the topping, stir the amaretto liqueur into the crème fraîche and spread over the cheesecake. Sprinkle the crushed amaretti cookies round the edge to decorate.

ricotta cheesecake

ingredients

SERVES 6–8

for the pastry

6 oz/175 g/1⅛ cups all-
  purpose flour, plus extra
  for dusting
3 tbsp. superfine sugar
salt
4 oz/115 g unsalted butter,
  chilled and diced
1 egg yolk

for the filling

1 lb/450 g ricotta cheese
4 fl oz/125 ml/½ cup heavy
  cream
2 eggs, plus 1 egg yolk
3 oz/85 g/⅜ cup superfine
  sugar
finely grated rind of 1 lemon
finely grated rind of 1 orange

method

To make the pastry, sift the flour with the sugar and a pinch of salt onto a counter and make a well in the center. Add the diced butter and egg yolk to the well and, using your fingertips, gradually work in the flour mixture until fully incorporated.

Gather up the dough and knead very lightly. Cut off about one-quarter, wrap in plastic wrap, and let chill in the refrigerator. Press the remaining dough into the base of a 9-inch/23-cm tart pan with removable sides. Let chill for 30 minutes.

To make the filling, beat the ricotta with the cream, eggs and extra egg yolk, sugar, lemon rind, and orange rind. Cover with plastic wrap and set aside in the refrigerator until required.

Prick the base of the pastry shell all over with a fork. Line with foil, fill with pie weights, and bake blind in a preheated oven, 375°F/190°C, for 15 minutes.

Remove the pastry shell from the oven and take out the foil and pie weights. Stand the pan on a wire rack and set aside to cool.

Spoon the ricotta mixture into the pastry shell and level the surface. Roll out the reserved pastry on a lightly floured counter and cut it into strips. Arrange the strips over the filling in a lattice pattern, brushing the overlapping ends with water so that they stick.

Bake in the preheated oven, 375°F, for 30–35 minutes, until the top of the cheesecake is golden and the filling has set. Let cool on a wire rack before lifting off the side of the pan. Cut into wedges to serve.

almond cake

ingredients

SERVES 12–14

butter, for greasing

3 eggs, separated

5 oz/140 g/5/8 cup superfine
  sugar

2 oz/55 g/3/8 cup potato flour

5 oz/140 g/1 cup almonds,
  blanched, peeled, and
  chopped finely

finely grated rind of 1 orange

41/4 oz/135 ml/generous
  1/2 cup orange juice

salt

confectioners' sugar, for dusting

method

Generously grease a round 8-inch/20-cm cake pan with removeable sides. Beat the egg yolks with the sugar in a medium bowl until pale and thick and the mixture leaves a ribbon trail when the whisk is lifted. Stir in the potato flour, almonds, orange rind, and orange juice.

Whisk the egg whites with a pinch of salt in another bowl until stiff. Gently fold the whites into the egg yolk mixture.

Pour the mixture into the pan and bake in a preheated oven, 325°F/170°C, for 50–60 minutes, until golden and just firm to the touch. Turn out onto a wire rack to cool. Sift over a little confectioners' sugar to decorate before serving.

tuscan christmas cake

ingredients

SERVES 12–14

4 oz/115 g/generous 3/4 cup
hazelnuts

4 oz/115 g/generous 3/4 cup
almonds

3 oz/85 g/1/2 cup candied
peel

2 oz/55 g/1/3 cup dried
apricots, chopped finely

2 oz/55 g/1/3 cup candied
pineapple, chopped finely

grated rind of 1 orange

2 oz/55 g/scant 1/2 cup all-
purpose flour

2 tbsp. unsweetened cocoa

1 tsp. ground cinnamon

1/4 tsp. ground coriander

1/4 tsp. freshly grated nutmeg

1/4 tsp. ground cloves

4 oz/115 g/generous 1/2 cup
superfine sugar

6 oz/175 g/1/2 cup honey

confectioners' sugar,
to decorate

method

Line an 8-inch/20-cm cake pan with removeable
sides with parchment paper. Spread out the hazelnuts
on a baking sheet and toast in a preheated oven,
350°F/180°C, for 10 minutes, until golden brown.
Pour them onto a dish towel and rub off the skins.
Meanwhile, spread out the almonds on a baking sheet
and toast in the oven for 10 minutes, until golden.
Watch carefully after 7 minutes because they can burn
easily. Reduce the oven temperature to 300°F. Chop all
the nuts and place in a large bowl.

Add the candied peel, apricots, pineapple, and orange
rind to the nuts and mix well. Sift together the flour,
unsweetened cocoa, cinnamon, coriander, nutmeg,
and cloves into the bowl and mix well.

Put the sugar and honey into a pan and set over low heat,
stirring, until the sugar has dissolved. Bring to a boil and
cook for 5 minutes, until thickened and starting to darken.
Stir the nut mixture into the pan and remove from the heat.

Spoon the mixture into the prepared cake pan and level
the surface with the back of a damp spoon. Bake in the
oven for 1 hour, then transfer to a wire rack to cool in
the pan.

Carefully remove the cake from the pan and peel off the
parchment paper. Just before serving, dredge the top
with confectioners' sugar. Cut into thin wedges to serve.

chestnut & chocolate terrine

ingredients

SERVES 6

7 fl oz/200 ml//³/₄ cup heavy
   cream
4 oz/115 g semisweet
   chocolate, melted
   and cooled
3¹/₂ fl oz/100 ml/generous
   ¹/₃ cup rum
1 package rectangular, plain,
   sweet cookies
8 oz/225 g canned sweetened
   chestnut purée
unsweetened cocoa,
   for dusting
confectioners' sugar,
   to decorate

method

Line a 1-lb/450-g loaf pan with plastic wrap. Place the cream in a bowl and whip lightly until soft peaks form. Using a spatula, fold in the cooled chocolate.

Place the rum in a shallow dish. Lightly dip 4 cookies into the rum and arrange on the bottom of the pan. Repeat with 4 more cookies. Spread half the chocolate cream over the cookies. Make another layer of 8 cookies dipped in rum and spread over the chestnut purée, followed by another layer of cookies. Spread over the remaining chocolate cream and top with a final layer of cookies. Cover with plastic wrap and let chill for 8 hours, or preferably overnight.

Turn the terrine out onto a large serving dish. Dust with unsweetened cocoa. Cut strips of paper and place these randomly on top of the terrine. Sift over confectioners' sugar. Carefully remove the paper. To serve, dip a sharp knife in hot water, dry it, and use it to cut the terrine into slices.

tiramisù

ingredients

SERVES 8

butter, for greasing

3 eggs

5 oz/140 g/3/4 cup golden
superfine sugar

31/2 oz/90 g/2/3 oz self-rising
flour

1 tbsp. unsweetened cocoa

5 fl oz/150 ml/2/3 cup cold
black coffee

2 tbsp. rum

2 tsp. unsweetened cocoa,
to decorate

filling

13 oz/375 g/15/8 cups
mascarpone cheese

8 fl oz/225 ml/1 cup fresh
custard

2 oz/55 g/1/4 cup golden
superfine sugar

31/2 oz/100 g semisweet
chocolate, grated

method

Preheat the oven to 350°F/180°C. To make the cake, grease an 8-inch/20-cm round cake pan with butter and line with parchment paper. Place the eggs and sugar in a large bowl and beat together until thick and light. Sift the flour and unsweetened cocoa over the batter and fold in gently. Spoon the batter into the prepared pan and bake in the oven for 30 minutes, or until the cake springs back when pressed gently in the center. Let stand in the tin for 5 minutes, then turn out onto a wire rack to cool.

Place the black coffee and rum in a bowl or cup, mix together and set aside. To make the filling, place the mascarpone cheese in a large bowl and beat until soft. Stir in the custard, then gradually add the sugar, beating constantly. Stir in the grated chocolate.

Cut the cake horizontally into 3 layers and place 1 layer on a serving plate. Sprinkle with one-third of the coffee mixture, then cover with one-third of the mascarpone mixture. Repeat the layers, finishing with a topping of the mascarpone mixture. Let chill in the refrigerator for 3 hours. Sift over the unsweetened cocoa before serving.

italian chocolate christmas pudding

ingredients

SERVES 10

butter, for greasing

4 oz/115 g/^{1}/$_2$ cup mixed
    candied fruit, chopped

2 oz/55 g/^{1}/$_3$ cup raisins

grated rind of ^{1}/$_2$ orange

3 tbsp. orange juice

3 tbsp. light cream

12 oz/350 g semisweet
    chocolate, chopped

4 oz/115 g/^{1}/$_2$ cup
    cream cheese

4 oz/115 g amaretti cookies,
    broken into coarse pieces

to serve

4 fl oz/125 ml/^{1}/$_2$ cup
    whipping cream

2 tbsp. amaretto liqueur

1 oz/25 g semisweet
    chocolate, grated

method

Grease a 3^1/$_2$-cup/850-ml ovenproof bowl with butter. Place the candied fruit, raisins, orange rind, and juice in a bowl and mix together. Put the light cream and chocolate in a pan and heat gently until the chocolate has melted. Stir until smooth, then stir in the fruit mixture. Let cool.

Place the cream cheese and a little of the chocolate mixture in a large bowl and beat together until smooth, then stir in the remaining chocolate mixture. Stir in the broken amaretti cookies. Pour into the prepared bowl, cover with plastic wrap and let chill in the refrigerator overnight.

To serve, turn the pudding out onto a chilled serving plate. Pour the whipping cream into a bowl and add the amaretto liqueur. Whip lightly until slightly thickened. Pour some of the cream over the pudding and sprinkle grated chocolate over the top. Serve with the remaining cream.

sicilian
ice cream cake

ingredients

SERVES 4

for the Genoa sponge cake

6 eggs, separated

7 oz/200 g/1 cup superfine sugar

3 oz/85 g/generous 1/2 cup self-rising flour

3 oz/85 g/generous 1/2 cup cornstarch

for the filling

1 lb 2 oz/500 g ricotta cheese

7 oz/200 g/1 cup superfine sugar

1 pint/600 ml/2 1/2 cups Maraschino liqueur

3 oz/85 g/ unsweetened chocolate

7 oz/200 g/generous 1 cup mixed candied peel, diced

1/2 pint/300 ml/1 1/4 cups heavy cream

to decorate

glacé cherries, angelica, candied peel, and slivered almonds

method

First, line a 10-inch/25-cm cake pan with removeable sides with parchment paper for the sponge cake.

Beat the egg yolks with the sugar until pale and frothy. In a separate, spotlessly clean bowl, whisk the whites until stiff peaks form. Gently fold the whites into the egg yolk mixture with a figure-eight action.

Sift together the flour and cornstarch into a bowl, then sift into the egg mixture and gently fold in. Pour the mixture into the cake pan and level the surface. Bake in a preheated oven, 350°F/180°C, for 30 minutes, until springy to the touch of a fingertip. Turn out onto a wire rack, remove the lining paper, and let cool completely.

For the filling, combine the ricotta, sugar, and 14 fl oz/400 ml/1 3/4 cups of the Maraschino in a bowl, beating well. Chop the chocolate with a knife and stir it into the mixture with the candied peel.

Cut the sponge cake into strips about 1/2 inch/1.25 cm wide and use some of it to line the bottom and sides of a 2-lb/900-g loaf pan. Set aside the remaining slices.

Spoon the ricotta mixture into the pan and level the surface. Cover with the reserved sponge cake. Drizzle the remaining Maraschino over the top, then chill overnight.

Run a round-bladed knife round the sides of the pan and turn out onto a serving plate. Whisk the cream until stiff and coat the top and sides of the cake. Decorate with the cherries, angelica, candied peel, and almonds.

lemon granita

ingredients

SERVES 4

16 fl oz/450 ml/2 cups water
4 oz/115 g/generous 1/2 cup
    white granulated sugar
8 fl oz/225 ml/1 cup lemon
    juice
grated rind of 1 lemon

method

Heat the water in a heavy-bottom pan over low heat.
Add the sugar and stir until it has completely dissolved.
Bring to a boil, remove the pan from the heat, and set
the syrup aside to cool.

Stir the lemon juice and rind into the syrup. Pour the
mixture into a freezerproof container and place in the
freezer for 3–4 hours.

To serve, remove the container from the freezer and dip
the base into hot water. Turn out the ice block and chop
coarsely, then place in a food processor and process
until it forms small crystals (granita means "granular").
Spoon into sundae glasses and serve immediately.

zucotto

ingredients

SERVES 6

4 oz/115 g soft margarine,
plus extra for greasing
3 1/2 oz/100 g/scant 2/3 cup
self-rising flour
2 tbsp. unsweetened cocoa
1/2 tsp. baking powder
4 oz/155 g/generous 1/2 cup
golden superfine sugar
2 eggs, beaten
3 tbsp. brandy
2 tbsp. Kirsch

filling

10 fl oz/300 ml/1 1/4 cups
heavy cream
1 oz/25 g/1/4 cup
confectioners' sugar, sifted
2 oz/55 g/1/4 cup toasted
almonds, chopped
8 oz/225 g black cherries, pitted
2 oz/55 g semisweet
chocolate, finely chopped

to decorate

1 tbsp. unsweetened cocoa
1 tbsp. confectioners' sugar
fresh cherries

method

Preheat the oven to 375°F/190°C. Grease a 12 x 9inch/ 30 x 23-cm jelly roll pan with margarine and line with parchment paper. Sift the flour, cocoa, and baking powder into a bowl. Add the sugar, margarine, and eggs. Beat together until well mixed, then spoon into the prepared pan. Bake in the preheated oven for 15–20 minutes, or until well risen and firm to the touch. Let stand in the pan for 5 minutes, then turn out onto a wire rack to cool.

Using the rim of a 5-cup/1.2-litre ovenproof bowl as a guide, cut a circle from the cake and set aside. Line the bowl with plastic wrap. Use the remaining cake, cutting it as necessary, to line the bowl. Place the brandy and Kirsch in a small bowl and mix together. Sprinkle over the cake, including the reserved circle.

To make the filling, pour the cream into a separate bowl and add the confectioners' sugar. Whip until thick, then fold in the almonds, cherries, and chocolate. Fill the sponge mold with the cream mixture and press the cake circle on top. Cover with a plate and a weight, and let chill in the refrigerator for 6–8 hours, or overnight. When ready to serve, turn the zucotto out onto a serving plate. Decorate with cocoa and confectioners' sugar, sifted over in alternating segments, and a few cherries.

chestnut mousse

ingredients

SERVES 6

1 lb/450 g sweet chestnuts

1/2 pint/300 ml/1 1/4 cups milk

1 bay leaf

2-in/2.5-cm cinnamon stick

6 oz/175 g/generous 3/4 cup
    superfine sugar

2 large eggs yolks

1/2 tsp. vanilla extract

4 tbsp. dark rum

1/4 pint/150 ml/2/3 cup
    heavy cream, plus extra
    to decorate

butter, for greasing

method

Use a sharp knife to cut a slit in the rounded side of the shell of each chestnut, then place them in large pan. Add cold water to cover and bring to a boil. Boil for about 5 minutes, then remove with a slotted spoon. When cool enough to handle, but still warm, remove the shells. The inner skins should easily peel off at the same time.

Place the chestnuts in a clean, heavy-bottom pan, pour in the milk and add the bay leaf, cinnamon, and half the superfine sugar. Bring to a boil, stirring to dissolve the sugar. Reduce the heat, cover and let simmer gently, stirring occasionally, for about 40 minutes, until the chestnuts are very tender. Remove the pan from the heat and set aside to cool.

Remove and discard the bay leaf and cinnamon stick from the pan and transfer the contents to a food processor or blender. Process to a smooth purée.

Beat the egg yolks with the remaining sugar until pale and fluffy and the whisk leaves a trail when lifted. Stir in the vanilla extract and rum, then gently fold in the chestnut purée.

Whip the cream in a separate bowl until it forms stiff peaks. Gently fold it into the chestnut mixture.

Lightly grease 6 individual ovenproof molds or ramekins with butter and spoon the mixture into them. Stand the molds on a baking sheet and bake in a preheated oven, 350°F/180°C, for 10–15 minutes, until just set.

Set the molds aside to cool to room temperature before serving. Alternatively, cover and chill until required. To serve, turn out the molds onto individual plates and pipe a border of whipped cream around the base of each one.

zabaglione

ingredients

SERVES 4

4 egg yolks

2¹/₄ oz/60 g/¹/₃ cup
　　superfine sugar

5 tbsp. Marsala

amaretti cookies, to serve

method

Whisk the egg yolks with the sugar in a heatproof bowl or, if you have one, the top of a double boiler for about 1 minute.

Gently whisk in the Marsala. Set the bowl over a pan of barely simmering water or put the top of the double boiler on its bottom filled with barely simmering water, and whisk vigorously for 10–15 minutes, until thick, creamy and foamy.

Immediately pour into serving glasses and serve with amaretti cookies.

chocolate zabaglione

ingredients

SERVES 4

4 egg yolks

4 tbsp. superfine sugar

1³/₄ oz/50 g semisweet
    chocolate

4 fl oz/125 ml¹/₂ cup Marsala
    wine

unsweetened cocoa, for
    dusting

amaretti cookies, to serve

method

Place the egg yolks and superfine sugar in a large glass bowl and, using an electric whisk, whisk together until the mixture is very pale.

Grate the chocolate finely and, using a spatula, fold into the egg mixture. Fold the Marsala wine into the chocolate mixture.

Place the bowl over a pan of gently simmering water and set the electric whisk on the lowest speed or swap to a balloon whisk. Cook gently, whisking constantly, until the mixture thickens. Do not overcook or the mixture will curdle.

Spoon the hot mixture into 4 warmed glass dishes or coffee cups and dust with cocoa. Serve as soon as possible, while it is warm, light, and fluffy, with amaretti cookies.

mascarpone creams

ingredients

SERVES 4

4 oz/115 g amaretti cookies, crushed

4 tbsp. amaretto or Maraschino

4 eggs, separated

2 oz/55 g/generous 1/4 cup superfine sugar

8 oz/225 g/1 cup mascarpone cheese

toasted slivered almonds, to decorate

method

Place the amaretti crumbs in a bowl, add the amaretto or Maraschino, and set aside to soak.

Meanwhile, beat the egg yolks with the superfine sugar until pale and thick. Fold in the mascarpone and soaked cookie crumbs.

Whisk the egg white in a separate, spotlessly clean bowl until stiff, then gently fold into the cheese mixture. Divide the mascarpone cream among serving dishes and let chill for 1–2 hours. Sprinkle with toasted slivered almonds just before serving.

chilled chocolate dessert

ingredients

SERVES 4–6

8 oz/225 g/1 cup mascarpone cheese

2 tbsp. finely ground coffee beans

1 oz/25 g/1/4 cup confectioners' sugar

3 oz/85 g unsweetened chocolate, grated finely

12 fl oz/350 ml/1 1/2 cups heavy cream, plus extra to decorate

Marsala, to serve

method

Beat the mascarpone with the coffee and confectioners' sugar until thoroughly combined.

Set aside 4 teaspoons of the grated chocolate and stir the remainder into the cheese mixture with 5 tablespoons of the unwhipped cream.

Whisk the remaining cream until it forms soft peaks. Stir 1 tablespoon of the mascarpone mixture into the cream to slacken it, then fold the cream into the remaining mascarpone mixture with a figure-eight action.

Spoon the mixture into a freezerproof container and place in the freezer for about 3 hours.

To serve, scoop the chocolate dessert into sundae glasses and drizzle with a little Marsala. Top with the extra cream, whipped, and decorate with the reserved grated chocolate. Serve immediately.

cappuccino soufflé puddings

ingredients

SERVES 4

butter, for greasing

2 tbsp. golden superfine sugar, plus extra for coating

6 tbsp. whipping cream

2 tsp. instant espresso coffee granules

2 tbsp. Kahlúa

3 large eggs, separated, plus 1 extra egg white

$5^1/2$ oz/150 g semisweet chocolate, melted and cooled

unsweetened cocoa, for dusting

vanilla ice cream or cookies, to serve

method

Preheat the oven to 375°F/190°C. Lightly grease the sides of 6 x $^3/4$ -cup/175-ml ramekins with butter and coat with superfine sugar. Place the ramekins on a baking sheet.

Place the cream in a small, heavy-bottom pan and heat gently. Stir in the coffee until it has dissolved, then stir in the Kahlúa. Divide the coffee mixture between the prepared ramekins.

Place the egg whites in a clean, greasefree bowl and whisk until soft peaks form, then gradually whisk in the sugar until stiff but not dry. Stir the egg yolks and melted chocolate together in a separate bowl, then stir in a little of the whisked egg whites. Gradually fold in the remaining egg whites.

Divide the mixture between the dishes. Bake in the preheated oven for 15 minutes, or until just set. Dust with unsweetened cocoa and serve immediately with vanilla ice cream or cookies.

coffee panna cotta with chocolate sauce

ingredients

SERVES 6

oil, for brushing

1 pint/600 ml/2½ cups heavy cream

1 vanilla bean

2 oz/55 g/generous ¼ cup golden superfine sugar

2 tsp. instant espresso coffee granules, dissolved in 4 tbsp. water

2 tsp. powdered gelatin

chocolate-covered coffee beans, to serve

sauce

5 fl oz/150 ml/⅔ cup light cream

2 oz/55 g semisweet chocolate, melted

method

Lightly brush 6 x ⅔ -cup/150-ml molds with oil. Place the cream in a pan. Split the vanilla bean and scrape the black seeds into the cream. Add the vanilla bean and the sugar, then heat gently until almost boiling. Strain the cream into a heatproof bowl and set aside. Place the coffee in a small heatproof bowl, sprinkle on the gelatin and let stand for 5 minutes, or until spongy. Set the bowl over a pan of gently simmering water until the gelatin has dissolved.

Stir a little of the reserved cream into the gelatin mixture, then stir the gelatin mixture into the remainder of the cream. Divide the mixture between the prepared molds and let cool, then let chill in the refrigerator for 8 hours, or overnight.

To make the sauce, place one-quarter of the cream in a bowl and stir in the melted chocolate. Gradually stir in the remaining cream, reserving 1 tablespoon. To serve the panna cotta, dip the base of the molds briefly into hot water and turn out onto 6 dessert plates. Pour the chocolate cream round. Dot drops of the reserved cream onto the sauce and feather it with a toothpick. Decorate with chocolate-covered coffee beans and serve.

marsala cherries

ingredients

SERVES 4

5 oz/140 g/5/8 cup
   superfine sugar
thinly pared rind of 1 lemon
2-in/5-cm piece of
   cinnamon stick
8 fl oz/225 ml/1 cup water
8 fl oz/225 ml/1 cup Marsala
2 lb /900 g Morello cherries,
   pitted
1/4 pint/150 ml/2/3 cup
   heavy cream

method

Put the sugar, lemon rind, cinnamon stick, water, and Marsala in a heavy-bottom pan and bring to a boil, stirring constantly. Reduce the heat and let simmer for 5 minutes. Remove the cinnamon stick.

Add the Morello cherries, cover, and let simmer gently for 10 minutes. Using a slotted spoon, transfer the cherries to a bowl.

Return the pan to the heat and bring to a boil over high heat. Boil for 3–4 minutes, until thick and syrupy. Pour the syrup over the cherries and set aside to cool, then chill for at least 1 hour.

Whisk the cream until stiff peaks form. Divide the cherries and syrup between 4 individual dishes or glasses, top with the cream, and serve.